End

When I first met Cheryl, we [...] *Team." The gospel was a key* [...] *'teammate' Chuck. Those whose lives intersected with hers are blessed from the insights shared in her writings, but also by seeing the gospel lived out daily. You will be enriched, energized, and encouraged as you read her ponderings!*

Rev. Kevin Haley

There isn't anything which touches my life that hasn't passed through the hand of God first. As a Christian, I believe that to be true. Not only in the circumstances of my life but also in the people who He causes to cross my path. Nothing in the Lord's plan is random. So it is with the intersection of my believer's journey with that of Cheryl Abrams Hildbold.

Cheryl was the wife of my childhood friend, Chuck. As a partner in his ministry as a United Methodist pastor, she witnessed the gamut of circumstances and peoples. Cheryl was unfailingly positive that their calling together as a ministering couple was just that. A calling. For both of them. With intentional living out of her faith, Cheryl demonstrated again and again the authenticity of her intimate relationship with Jesus Christ.

As in the first collection of her musings, "Ponderings from the Pastor's Partner", the book which you are holding is chock full of insights, humor and thoughtful observances. Cheryl's gift for writing impactful articles will most certainly cause your spirit to settle and your soul to sing. The eternal truths which guided Cheryl still speak though her lyrical voice cannot.

May the Lord establish His truth in your life through the words of His humble servant, Cheryl.

Deb Andrison

I had the pleasure of knowing Cheryl while I was living in Tionesta, PA. Chuck was the new pastor of the Methodist Church in town and I was the choir director. Even though Cheryl was a couple of years younger than me, I felt as though I was always learning from her; from the way she hosted the dinners at the parsonage (Chuck mentioned these in the first book), to the way she used her beautiful voice to worship God, to having a personal relationship with our Lord, to being a great partner to Chuck, to being a loving mother to Charlie (and later Carrie, Caitlin and Caleb).

The first book, "Ponderings from the Pastor's Partner" gave such wonderful glimpses into Cheryl's everyday life and her many thoughts and feelings. The "Light" of Christ that shined through Cheryl was always a beacon for others to follow. Not only did she talk the talk but she walked the walk as well, and many were drawn to the "Light" because of her. I was blessed to have known her and you will be blessed by reading her "Ponderings."

Bonnie Champion

Having first met Cheryl and Chuck on a lay witness mission years ago in Tionesta, right from the beginning, there was something warm and special about Cheryl. Over the many years, I've looked forward to the newsletters arriving and reading the Ponderings from the Pastor's Partner. Cheryl would write in the monthly newsletter and I always gleaned wise words and tips through Cheryl's writings and insight. I used to think, if I ever became a Pastor's wife, I'd like to be like Cheryl. She was my mentor, constantly steadfast in her walk with Jesus. I was fortunate to spend time with Cheryl at the last annual conference held in Grove City. For that precious time together, I'm forever grateful. When the family decided to put together her second book of writings, it thrills me that Cheryl's words and wisdom, from knowing and applying Jesus in her everyday life, would keep on blessing others. Cheryl, you're so missed. I'm glad your writing is available for all to read.

Joslyn Pawloski

Grab a latte or brew a cup of tea, settle down in your favorite chair, and prepare to have your heart be touched. Cheryl's first book, "Ponderings From the Pastor's Partner," was a whimsical, soul-stirring collection of anecdotes that could have you chuckling one moment and praying prayers of thanksgiving the next. As friends who first met Cheryl and Chuck during our college days together, it was a delight to watch Cheryl unveil her heart in the pages of her book. Life in the parsonage is not always easy, but as Cheryl so eloquently shares, no matter where we find ourselves in life, God always has lessons for us to help us grow and continue His work. Whether you read each pondering as a daily devotional or read her book in one sitting, you will be assured that God loves you and that in even the most mundane of life's circumstances, you can see the hand and lessons of God. We have no doubt that this second book of "Ponderings" will touch many hearts as well.

Rev. John & Anne Phipps

Cheryl and I met at a Lay Witness Weekend in the late 80's through a mutual friend. We became friends almost immediately. It was like she was my sister and of course we were siblings in Jesus Christ. She talked about her family and it was like I knew each of them personally from listening to her talk. She had a beautiful singing voice that was easy to listen to. I got to meet her family when I was selected for the Lay Witness team at Chuck's church in East Brady.

I will always cherish the friendship that grew between our families. My hope and prayer would be that every person reading this second book will get to know the wonderful Christian that Cheryl always was. God calls us to be His ambassadors here on earth and Cheryl represented Him in ways that most of us can only hope to do. Through her ponderings she can still be the Lord's witness.

Norm Kaufman

The first time I met Cheryl was at a Clergy Spouse Retreat in the '90's. She and I were both young mothers with four or more children. I remember Cheryl's beautiful smile and energetic spirit. She impressed me as a mom who had it all together. Everyone there seemed to know Cheryl and her magnetizing personality. As the years went by, I truly looked forward to reuniting with her at the next retreat and catching up on what happened in our lives. You could always spot her quickly if you listened for the laughter. There was no doubt that Cheryl knew Jesus as her Savior. Her witness by her talk and her walk was obvious. We lost track of each other when she was diagnosed with cancer and no longer attended retreats and it was in the last three years of her life that we connected more often including spending time at a few conferences at the Ark in Kentucky. I am grateful to God to have known her.

Cathie Lester

We have turned a small bedroom into our prayer room and have a glassed-in bookcase where I keep Cheryl's book. When I think of Cheryl, I like to picture her enjoying riding her beloved bicycle throughout Heaven, often stopping to chat with Jesus, friends, and family who have preceded her to Heaven. She is enjoying perfect health and I am sure she often peaks through the clouds to see how Chuck and her family are doing. Her first book is such an inspiration and I can't wait to read this second edition of "ponderings." You will be blessed by her love for Jesus!

Maggie & Tommy Eldridge

I only knew Cheryl for a much shorter time than most but that did not keep me from finding the joy in her life even while battling the cancer in her body. She was always smiling and filled with the heart of Jesus. Her spirit was contagious and her love of her Lord and her family emulated from that Spirit that directed her life. She was the essence of Christ.

Pastor Denton Lester

Steve and I have known Chuck and Cheryl for years as we developed websites for the churches they served. Through the years, what started as a business relationship, grew into a wonderful friendship, a true blessing that holds a very special place in our hearts.

Flashback to several years ago and our paths took an unseen twist. Unseen by us, but fully known by God. Within a couple weeks of each other, Cheryl began her journey with cancer and I was attacked by a Great Dane. An attack that left puncture wounds and crush wounds to my face and inner thigh; wounds that would lead to months of infection and multiple surgeries and subsequent weeks and months of questioning God. It was in these moments that God clearly used Cheryl to be the light in the darkness. Early in her battle Cheryl created pages of scriptures that meant something to her and she sent those pages to me. Each day I read them and each day my hope grew and my faith was strengthened. To some, those pages of scripture were simply words on paper. But to me, they became my lifeline, the path to a deeper, stronger walk with God. Those scriptures, but more specifically, Cheryl, taught me that even in times of struggle, even in the times of suffering, God is still there and He still cares. Cheryl was the vessel through which Jesus' light shined in my darkness, and my hope for tomorrow. Regardless of what Cheryl went through, she still shared her faith and offered Jesus to anyone who didn't know Him and to those who did, like me. Her faith taught me that no matter what we are going through, no matter the struggle, it can be used for good. We can struggle but we don't have to become that struggle. We can still witness for God and we can witness well.

Our lives are forever changed and blessed to have known and loved Cheryl. Each "Ponderings" is a piece of her that lives on and a legacy of faith and love that nothing can extinguish!

MaryJo Young

More Ponderings from the Pastor's Partner

Cheryl Abrams Hildbold

Cover Photography taken by Cheryl A. Hildbold

Editing and formatting of this book provided by YCS Global, LLC, owners Steven & MaryJo Young. www.YCSGlobal.com.

ISBN: 978-1-66786-207-1

Table of Contents

Articles (Continued)

Articles (Continued)

Articles (Continued)

Foreword

*He who finds a wife finds what is good and
receives favor from the Lord. (Proverbs 18:22)*

*She speaks with wisdom and faithful instruction is her heritage.
She watches over the affairs of her household and does not eat
the bread of idleness. Her children arise and call her blessed; her
husband also, and he praises her: "Many women do noble things,
but you surpass them all." (Proverbs 31:26-29)*

As you read the following pages of articles from previous church newsletters, in other words, Cheryl's "ponderings", you will be very much aware that the words of the verses from the Book of Proverbs written above, are very true.

Cheryl grew up in Ithaca, New York. She was involved with the swim team in high school and, more importantly, her church and its youth group where she developed a strong and lasting commitment to Jesus Christ.

Cheryl attended Grove City College and earned her B.A. in Sociology. She loved to sing and play her guitar and that was where I first met her. We began dating five months later, were engaged 21 months later, and were married three weeks after she graduated, which was after I had completed my first year in Seminary. We were married in Harbison Chapel on the college campus and had wedding pictures taken in the garden outside of the Chapel. Because of the generosity of some good friends, there is a plaque in memory of Cheryl in that garden. It is, indeed, a very special place! (See photo on page 42)

Cheryl was kind and genuinely cared for other people. She had a pure heart and she instilled that virtue into the lives of our children.

Cheryl took care of our family. Her wisdom with regards to finances, the relationships with church members, family issues, and Scriptural integrity was invaluable. You will read of the love our children have for her and the love she wrote about and gave to each of them. And the grandchildren? Oh my! What a special love they had in her heart.

A number of years ago, we asked our children to forego gifts for our birthdays. Instead, we asked each of them to write us letters. Those letters are included in this book. You will also read the very touching words from our son Charlie, words that were shared during her memorial service. (Things We Learned From Mom: Page 90)

Cheryl loved to travel and was captivated by the beauty of God's creation. She was meticulous in planning our trips. The adventures we shared: The exhilarating (and terrifying) drive up Mount Washington in New Hampshire and the winding drive along the Needles Highway in South Dakota. The awe we experienced at the Grand Canyon or standing by the giant sequoias and the day we were the first to experience the sunrise in the United States on Cadillac Mountain in Maine. From the Atlantic Ocean to the Pacific Ocean, Cheryl loved seeing God's creativity. If there was any possibility of climbing a lighthouse, that was also included as part of our travels.

Cheryl loved riding her bicycle whether it was on the bike trail or simply riding it to work at the church. We were blessed to live close enough to the trails that we could take part of an afternoon and go biking.

Cheryl was my wife six days shy of 41 years. I knew her better than anyone and she was without exception, the most Christ-like person I have ever known. We took our wedding vows very seriously. "To have and hold, for better or worse." And the "worse" part came when she was diagnosed with cancer in 2016. She battled for five years and as was said at her memorial service, "Cheryl did not lose her life to cancer.

Cancer did not have the power to rob her of her life. Her life already belonged to Jesus. Cancer lost." It is an odd and unusual feeling not having her with me at the dinner table or on the couch or in the car. We were like the teeth in two gears and gears are not made to run by themselves. I miss her terribly yet I know without a doubt that we will be together again. The hope of heaven and the promise of new life because of trusting in Jesus and what He did on the cross, are all I need and all that anyone needs. That is the hope of this book.

As I have re-read her ponderings and the notes in her journals and her Bible, I was reminded of how much she talked about heaven. Even though she loved her life with us on earth, she so much looked forward to being with Jesus in eternity. And you will hear about Jesus all throughout these ponderings because He was the most important Person in her life.

So please read these ponderings with Jesus on your mind. Yes, you will get to know my sweet wife a little better, but please note that my prayer is that everything that is in these pages points to Jesus and the love that He freely gave to Cheryl and gives to each one of you reading this book.

Jesus, thank you for my wife. And Cheryl, in the meantime, until we meet again...I love you, Sweetie.

Chuck

My Personal Testimony

by Cheryl Abrams Hildbold

I was born into a home where my Dad was Catholic and my Mom was a former Baptist. When they married in 1949, they were going to alternate where they worshipped, but when my brother was born in 1950, we were a Catholic family. My sister was born in 1952 and I came along in 1958. We went to church every Sunday and said a memorized blessing before every dinner. At bed-time, I said another memorized prayer. I knew the story of Christmas and Easter and went to Catholic school through 4th grade...but there was never the mention of having a personal relationship with God.

My parents separated during the summer of 1967. I lived with my mom and my brother and my sister and since my mom had never turned Catholic, we stopped going to church. I also had to stop going to Catholic school because it was now going to cost us and we didn't have the money. So, I was adjusting to a new life without my dad and I was the new kid at a new school just trying to fit in.

My Mom remarried in 1970. My brother and sister no longer lived at home and I had to go to yet another new school. I was feeling very alone. I made some friends, but I always felt like I was trying to fit in. Most of these kids had gone to school together since kindergarten...I sort of felt like I was on the outside looking in.

On Easter Sunday, 1973, it was our turn to host the family meal. Our house was filled with Grandparents, Aunts, Uncles and Cousins...yet I still had a loneliness that I couldn't explain. I remember going outside and sitting on the porch and actually talking to God for the first time in my life...telling Him that I felt like something was missing in my life...not knowing that it was Him!

In the summer of 1973, I went to see the movie *Jesus Christ Superstar* and I was blown away. I saved my allowance and bought the record and listened to it over and over and over. I even recorded it onto a cassette tape so that I could carry it around and listen to it even when I wasn't home. In the late fall of 1973, I was walking up the road from our house, listening to JCS and crying. I felt lonelier than I ever had... despondent really. A car approached and it was my Uncle Howie on his way home from work. He asked me what was wrong and I told him that I was just lonely. He said, "I love you, honey and God loves you too and He is always with you." I had never heard that before...that God loved ME!

In the Spring of 1974, my parents and I had some friends that asked us to come to church with them. They asked us every week, but we always made up some excuse as to why we couldn't go. When we finally ran out of excuses, we told them that we would come...but that we were going to be shopping around for a church...just another excuse as to why we wouldn't be back for a 2nd visit! We went to a church in our old neighborhood... seeing people we hadn't seen for over 7 years...and it felt like coming home! Everyone

"I love you, honey and God loves you too and He is always with you."

was so welcoming and friendly. We knew we had found what we didn't even realize we were looking for...and we stayed! I got involved with the youth group and went to something called a "Coke Party" one Sunday afternoon. The youth leader stood up and talked about a relationship with Jesus Christ, which I expected to hear. But then a kid my own age stood up and told us that God loves us...the same thing my Uncle Howie had said. At that moment, I realized that this was what was missing in my life...the answer to my years of loneliness!

Let me back up just a bit. Remember how I said that I was always trying to fit in? Well, I was basically a "good kid". I didn't smoke or drink or swear. I didn't give my parents a hard time...but there's something I did that was worse than all of those things put together. I made someone feel worthless...on a regular basis. We had a fairly long bus ride to school. I was one of the first kids on and the bus was full by the time we got to school. One of the last students to get on the bus was a girl named Jackie. Jackie had a weight problem as well as some other problems that made her an undesirable seat mate for most of the kids. The bus always went around a big curve just before getting to Jackie's house and when it did, all the kids would spread out, making it look like their seats were full. Every day, Jackie would get on the bus and every day all the kids would look down...and every day, the bus driver had to make someone move over so that Jackie could sit down...every day...and I went right along with it...my way of trying to fit in!

Now back to the "Coke Party": I prayed the prayer that the leader told us to pray if we wanted to have a relationship with Jesus Christ...a relationship that would change our lives forever! The only thing was...after I prayed the prayer and opened my eyes...I didn't *feel* any different. The next day, Monday, I got up, got dressed, got on the bus, went around the curve before Jackie's house...and moved over, making room in my seat for her...and made eye contact with her, letting her know that she could sit with me...and my life was changed...just like that!

I gave my life to Jesus in March of 1974, even though I feel that God was calling to me long before that, and I have never regretted that decision. On the contrary...I've been blessed because of that decision. I've been married to a wonderful man of God for 40 years. We have 4 amazing children, 2 sons in law, a daughter in law and a daughter in law to-be who all love the Lord. We also have the privilege to be a positive influence for the Lord in the lives of our 8 grandchildren. Now, my life hasn't always been easy. Moving around as we do, I struggle with trying to fit in and often times feeling lonely...but never as I did before I knew Jesus...because He is always with me...and I know for a fact that He loves ME!

Three things that I would like you to take away from my story:

- ❖ Never give up on asking someone to church...eventually, they'll run out of excuses.

- ❖ Make sure that you are friendly and welcoming to the guests that we have here at our church.

- ❖ A good story always has to have a hero...and this one has two: Jackie for having the incredible courage to get on that bus every day and Jesus: the One who makes all things and all people new! Listen to God when He calls to you...He wants you to know that you are loved and that He wants to have a relationship with you...one that will change your life forever!

And one last thing...it's not enough to give your life to Christ, you need to make Him Lord of your life and do all you can to grow in your faith for the rest of your life.

Greatest Treasure

Life is funny! From the time we're born, we begin to accumulate things. Over the years, we get rid of some items...furniture that's worn out and old clothes that are out of style (or that don't fit!) ...usually replacing them with new ones...thus, not really getting rid of anything! I don't know about you, but as I get older, I have this growing sense of urgency to downsize...to lighten the load. Maybe it's because we've moved a lot and I'm tired of having so much stuff to pack...or maybe it's God's way of gradually helping me to let go of the material...making more room for the spiritual. At any rate, I find myself constantly evaluating our possessions...scrutinizing each item and trying to make a decision as to whether it should stay or go.

When Carrie got married and moved away, she took almost everything that was hers with her. Charlie and Caitlin, on the other hand, left most of their childhood possessions behind...and they call to me from the attic like the residents of Dr. Seuss' "Who-ville" saying, "We are here, we are here, we are here!" Caleb still lives home but has definitely outgrown some things...things like the Fisher-Price farm and the magnetic letters that stick to the fridge...and he's no longer interested in reading about the Berenstain Bears or playing Candy Land...but I'm trying to be cautious about getting rid of too much because I want our home to be a fun place for our granddaughter, Emily, to visit!

There are, however, certain things that I'm not ready to part with...things that have gone beyond being possessions...things that have become treasures...things like the Norman Rockwell picture hanging over our bed that Chuck painted for me before we were even married and the counted cross stitch sampler bearing our name that took me 14 months to complete. Most importantly, I'm not ready to part with the Bible that I've been using since I received it on my 28th birthday...the Bible that has scribble marks in the 5th chapter of Acts where Carrie got hold of a pen on the day that she was 20 months old...the same Bible that has a wrinkled page in the 8th chapter of Luke from the spray bottle that I was using to simulate the storm that Jesus calmed during Vacation Bible School...not to mention the many notes that I've taken in the margins and on just about every available blank space...the Bible that must stay in its zipper case because the cover has been hot-glued and taped back on!

Some things need to be gotten rid of, but there are some things that hopefully will never be gotten rid of...just passed on!

The girls like to "bicker" over who's going to get that picture over the bed...but I think the thing that they should all "bicker" over is that Bible...for that is my greatest treasure!

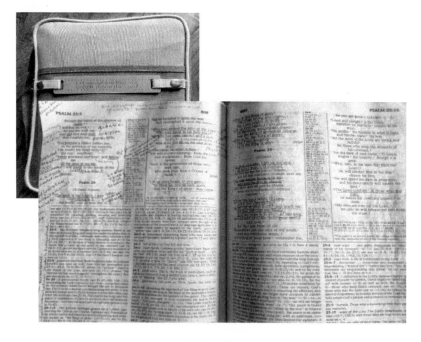

Our New Home

P eople are still asking, "How do you like your new home?", "Are you all settled in?", "How are the kids adjusting?" Now I can answer all of these questions with a resounding "FINE!", but for a while, that third question was a concern. The first two weeks that we were here, not a night went by without someone saying, "I wish we were back in East Brady." We had to keep reassuring them that "we're where God wants us to be now and we're all together as a family and everything will be fine." This nightly ritual gradually reduced to twice a week and now is non-existent. This is home!

This experience reminds me of the Israelites and Moses in the book of Exodus. The Israelites were always looking back, longing to return to the place they had called "home" for so many years. Moses' job was to convince them that God had a different plan in mind and that if they all stuck together and gave it some time, things would turn out fine.

God has a plan for each and every one of us. He wants to guide us through life, making our lives the best they can be with our ultimate destination being heaven. Unfortunately, we often find ourselves looking back, longing to stay somewhere when God is ready for us to move on. Our faith in God needs to be strong enough to enable us to trust our lives with Him – knowing that everything will turn out fine and someday, heaven will be home!

Cereal Gifts

I was recently putting away some groceries and as I found a place on the shelf for a new box of cereal, I noticed that they were advertising on the front that you should check inside the box to see if you won $100! I was amazed because I remember when it was a big deal to get a free ring or some other small toy inside the cereal box. Nowadays when they put something in the box, it is individually wrapped and located at the top of the box, but when I was a kid, the prize was not wrapped and it was hidden somewhere among the pieces of cereal and it was definitely my job to reach my grimy little hand down through the cereal in search of the coveted prize, after which the cereal was crushed and the box badly misshapen, but it was worth it! It occurred to me that the cereal companies have gotten a little out of control...or maybe it's just that people have come to expect so much more than they should!

As I think about the approaching Christmas season, I notice that things have gotten *more than a little* out of control and that we expect much more than we should. I remember when our kids were happy getting Tinker Toys and sticker books...and Christmas had a much slower pace when I was a kid...and God, who started this whole Christmas thing certainly intended for it to be low-key: He sent His Son, the King of Kings as a tiny baby born to a poor virgin in a manger.

Take some time this Christmas season to appreciate the simplicity of the Christmas story...go back to a time when things were not so out of control...when God was in control...because remember, He still is!

Digging Holes

We recently spent a few days at the beach...same beach we always go to...same beach we've taken all of our children to. Charlie always liked to build sandcastles. Carrie whiled away the hours digging for sand crabs. Caitlin would walk along the shore searching for seashells. This year, Caleb was the only one to go with us and guess how he spent his days...digging holes! Now, I'd like to tell you that these were special holes...dug-outs to be used in the midst of battle or hiding places for pirate treasure. But they were just holes...no steps, no windows, no tunnels...just holes. We could ask him to spend the day digging a hole at home and he would consider it a punishment! I can't think of anything else he would be so willing to do all day long...we had to force him to stop long enough to have something to eat!

I do need to mention that he wasn't digging alone...there were various cousins helping out with the project at one time or another...even his Dad and Uncle pitched in a little. One of the younger

"Do I look like I want to dig a hole?."

girls asked me if I wanted to help dig and I just smiled at her and asked if I looked like I wanted to dig a hole! (Well, that's a story for another time.) Anyway, I'm not so sure that Caleb would've been so eager to spend the day digging had he been all alone. It was the companionship that made it fun...the teamwork that made it worthwhile...just like life...just like the body of Christ. God promises that He will never leave us (Joshua 1:5), and that He will be with us always (Matthew

28:20). But He also encourages us to meet with one another (Hebrews 10:25), and to be there for each other in all aspects of life (Colossians 3 & 4).

Later this month, Caleb will be going on another trip with us...a mission trip with some folks from our church. He asked me what kinds of things we'll be doing and I told him that I really don't know...but I'm sure that the companionship will make it fun and that the teamwork will make it worthwhile and that God will be with us...and we will be blessed!

States and Capitals

When the kids were in school, I was always willing to help with homework. I remember going over the times tables and all kinds of spelling words. I remember filling out maps of the world and especially of the United States...and even learning their capitals!

One evening, Chuck and I were watching a rerun on TV and in the show, there was a challenge to name all 50 states in six minutes or less...so, naturally, I felt the urge to compete as well!

I had to try this more than once because even though most of the states came easily to me, I kept forgetting one or two...which was not acceptable!

I decided to write them all out, alphabetically, over and over until I learned them. Once that was accomplished, I decided that I should know their capitals as well...and so I listed the states followed by their capitals until I could get them all right without cheating.

Now I can write both lists proficiently, but I'm afraid that if I go too long without doing it, I'll forget again. So, a couple times a week, I write a new list, just to make sure that I remember what I so diligently learned.

In addition to helping the kids with their homework, I also helped them to memorize Scripture. When we introduced a new Scripture, we would write it on an index card and tape it to the wall. Every evening before bed, we would recite not only the verse they were working on, but the ones they had already learned so they wouldn't forget them.

If I can learn the states and their capitals, I can learn Scripture verses too...and so can you!

Alabama — Montgomery   Montana — Helena
Alaska — Juneau   Nebraska — Lincoln
Arizona — Phoenix   Nevada — Carson City
Arkansas — Little Rock   New Hampshire — Concord
California — Sacramento   New Jersey — Trenton
Colorado — Denver   New Mexico — Santa Fe
Connecticut — Hartford   New York — Albany
Delaware — Dover   N. Carolina — Raleigh
Florida — Tallahassee   N. Dakota — Bismark
Georgia — Atlanta   Ohio — Columbus
Hawaii — Honolulu   Oklahoma — Oklahoma City
Idaho — Boise   Oregon — Salem
Illinois — Springfield   Pennsylvania — Harrisburg
Indiana — Indianapolis   Rhode Island — Providence
Iowa — Des Moines   S. Carolina — Columbia
Kansas — Topeka   S. Dakota — Pierre
Kentucky — Frankfort   Tennessee — Nashville
Louisiana — Baton Rouge   Texas — Austin
Maine — Augusta   Utah — Salt Lake City
Maryland — Ana...
Massachusetts — ...
Michigan — La...
Minnesota — St...
Mississippi — Ja...
Missouri — Jeff...

A-5   B-4   C-6   D-3   F-1   H-4
I-1   J-3   L-3   M-3   N-1   O-2
P-3   R-2   S-6   T-3

Albany — New York   Jefferson City — Missouri
Annapolis — Maryland   Juneau — Alaska
Atlanta — Georgia   Lansing — Michigan
Augusta — Maine   Lincoln — Nebraska
Austin — Texas   Little Rock — Arkansas
Baton Rouge — Louisiana   Madison — Wisconsin
Bismarck — N. Dakota   Montgomery — Alabama
Boise — Idaho   Montpelier — Vermont
Boston — Massachusetts   Nashville — Tennessee
Carson City — Nevada   Oklahoma City — Oklahoma
Charleston — W. Virginia   Olympia — Washington
Cheyenne — Wyoming   Phoenix — Arizona
Columbia — S. Carolina   Pierre — S. Dakota
Columbus — Ohio   Providence — Rhode Island
Concord — N. Hampshire   Raleigh — N. Carolina
Denver — Colorado   Richmond — Virginia
Des Moines — Iowa   Sacramento — California
Dover — Delaware   Salem — Oregon
Frankfort — Kentucky   Salt Lake City — Utah
Harrisburg — Pennsylvania   Santa Fe — N. Mexico
Hartford — Connecticut   Springfield — Illinois
Helena — Montana   St. Paul — Minnesota
Honolulu — Hawaii   Tallahassee — Florida
Indianapolis — Indiana   Topeka — Kansas
Jackson — Mississippi   Trenton — N. Jersey

What Will They Catch?

Whenever someone has a new baby, what's the first thing we hear? "He has your eyes." "Look, she's got your smile." These are known as inherited traits. We can't choose what we inherit...it's bred into us from the time of conception, and the traits that we inherit play a major part in making us who we are.

However, not all traits are inherited. Some are learned or "caught" from those around us, usually those with whom we spend most of our time. This could mean parents, caregivers, friends or even TV. Obviously, these learned behaviors can be either good or bad...ones that we want to either reinforce or discourage. Our behavior is contagious. If we surround ourselves with people who have colds, we're more likely to catch that cold than if we are around healthy people. Just so, if we surround ourselves with people who complain or use foul language or are violent...well, you can make the analogy.

Deuteronomy 6:5-9 says, *"Love the Lord your God with all your heart and with all your soul and with all your strength. These commandments that I give you today are to be upon your hearts. Impress them on your children. Talk about them when you sit at home and when you walk along the road, when you lie down and when you get up. Tie them as symbols on your hands and bind them on your foreheads. Write them on the doorframes of your houses and on your gates."*

Our behavior is contagious! Let's not allow people to "catch" anything bad from us but let us put God's Word upon our hearts so that we can spread His love to those around us.

Paper Route Appreciation

Some of you are not aware that Charlie had his appendix removed the day before Easter. All went well. He was a good patient and is now back to school and all of his activities. Like most boys his age, Charlie is involved in sports, which he had to give up for a month. No swimming, no biking, no baseball!!! And, like a lot of boys his age, he has a paper route which he was unable to do for two weeks.

Now, giving up sports was a sacrifice on his part but the paper route affected someone else...ME! For two weeks, I was up at 6am rolling, wrapping, and delivering papers. There was one consolation in all of this...it got me out for my walk every day. But it also gave me an appreciation for the job that Charlie does. I was able to put this saying to the test, "Walk a mile in someone else's shoes..."

Having an appreciation for what someone else does is important but is it enough? The Apostle Paul says in 1 Thessalonians 5:11, "*Therefore, encourage one another and build each other up, just as in fact you are doing.*" It's not enough to think that someone does a good job...it's important to tell them, to encourage them.

Charlie also has several jobs at church. He sets up the overhead and screen for the praise songs and runs the overhead during that time of the service. He makes sure that the sound system is ready to tape the sermon and he even unlocks doors and turns on lights. We missed him on Easter Sunday. Many of us gained an appreciation for the various jobs that Charlie does each Sunday...but how many of us told him?

We need to encourage one another and build each other up. That's what Jesus would have us do.

Banana Bread

Yesterday, I decided to carry out what I'd been threatening to do for months-make banana bread. I don't make it very often because when I do, I make a lot! I proceeded to pull 30 bananas out of my freezer, leaving at least that many in there as well! I don't know about you, but quite often, our family doesn't finish the bunch of bananas that we are currently consuming. I'll buy a big bunch and, invariably, there's one or two left toward the end of the week (more brown than yellow) and so I throw them into the freezer. I've tried buying smaller bunches, but the same thing happens – it's like everyone's afraid to be the one to finish them off. It must stem from the same principle of eating the last cookie in the package and polishing off the last bit of orange juice in the carton.

Anyway, I filled the sink with these frozen, now completely brown masses and got to work. As unappetizing as an over-ripe banana appears, they seem like a delicacy compared with ones that have been frozen and thawed. Bananas in that state look absolutely disgusting – especially when they come out of the peel. It seems highly unlikely that they can be put to any good use. Many people probably throw them away, especially if they've tried freezing them...but that's what makes the banana bread so good!

Have you ever felt like an over-ripe banana? Hanging around...nobody seems to want you...waiting to be cast aside...useless...worthless. I guess that's how I was feeling last month: hence no article. In Jeremiah 29:11, God says, *"For I know the plans I have for you, plans to prosper you and not to harm you, plans to give you hope and a future."* God has a plan for each and every one of us, no matter how worthless we feel.

As I looked at that pile of bananas in my sink, I saw the possibility of all the wonderful bread they would make and I realized that when God looks at me, He sees all the possibilities of the wonderful things He can do through me.

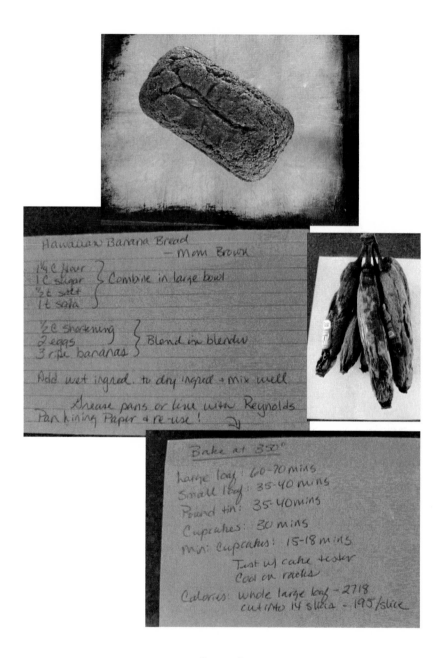

Hawaiian Banana Bread
— Mom Brown

1¾ C flour
1 C sugar
½ t salt   } Combine in large bowl
1 t soda

½ C Shortening
2 eggs   } Blend in blender
3 ripe bananas

Add wet ingred. to dry ingred + mix well

Grease pans or line with Reynolds Pan lining Paper & re-use!

Bake at 350°

Large loaf: 60-70 mins
Small loaf: 35-40 mins
Pound tin: 35-40 mins
Cupcakes: 30 mins
Mini cupcakes: 15-18 mins

Test w/ cake tester
Cool on racks
Calories: whole large loaf - 2718
          cut into 14 slices - 195/slice

Charlie's Birthday Letter

Happy Birthday Mom!

I was not sure exactly how I wanted to approach this, so I thought I'd do it on the fly! If I had to convey one feeling to you on your birthday, it would be a feeling of thanks. As I grow older and meet more and more people, I realize how special of a childhood we all had. The sacrifices that you made, not being able to work, driving us all over when Dad was working, giving up any free time or sleep you had to make sure we never had to go to day care, or have a babysitter is amazing. I also think about the fact that it wasn't until I was in my 20's that I even realized how much we struggled as a family growing up. It just never entered our minds as kids because you and Dad did such a great job making sure we had more than enough to be happy.

As much as we like to laugh now about the clothes you made, the fact that you had the ability and the talent to make us clothes is awesome! We never knew that they were different, or even really homemade, it was just the way it was. One of your best traits is your ability to provide clothes when we needed them, provide food every night for family dinners, provide your time at night to spend with us, and more!

I think about all of the times we used to go on trips, how you would prepare and make them as comfortable as possible and go over your giant list just to make sure that we didn't have to needlessly spend money on an already expensive vacation. I also think about how you taught us to sing as a family, and despite numerous protests from us, you made us get up and sing. We may never know if we had an effect on anyone at any of our "concerts" but what if we did? We could have possibly led someone to Christ, and it came from you and Dad forcing us to sing as a family -that's amazing! That love of singing was passed on to me, which led directly to me joining the Continentals. That trip ultimately made me what I am today. It showed me that people in other countries, with a completely different language, can still understand the language of Jesus. This probably leads to the best point I can make today.

The Bible tells us that we will know Christians by their fruit, and that we will ultimately be judged on how we've furthered the Kingdom. When your time comes, you can rest assured knowing that you have had an amazing impact on countless people, many of which you may have no idea about right now! Your choice to lead a Christ-centered life and raise your family that way has made ripples that could last for years. four kids, five grandchildren, all raised by your example. Think of future great grandchildren that you might never meet! Everyone we come in contact with, and ultimately minister to is being done because of your love and desire for the Lord. That fact alone would make for a great life for you...everything else you've done is just to enrich it!

I love the example you've set for me. I don't know what God's plan for me is but I'm blessed to actually have a family. I know now that I will never need to worry about how to treat my family or my wife, and I know exactly the type of woman I need – one just like you. I wish I could be with you on your birthday...I miss all of you so much!

Love you so much Mom!

Charlie

Gummies and the Treasure Hunt

Chuck and I like to include an all-natural gummy fiber in our daily regimen of vitamins. We used to always pick them up at Giant Eagle when they had a BOGO on that brand. Over the last year or so, we have been unable to find them and have resorted to purchasing them online at full price.

A couple of weeks ago, we were in a Giant Eagle and saw a bottle of our gummies. We were excited to find them but decided to wait for them to go on sale. Last Thursday, I was in our local Giant Eagle and discovered that they were indeed half price. There was only one bottle, but I picked it up and upon returning home, I informed Chuck that within the next week, we had to get to as many Giant Eagles as we could, to find as many of these gummies as we were able. It was like a treasure hunt!

"Do not store up for yourselves treasures on earth... but store up for yourselves treasure in heaven... for where your treasure is, there your heart will be also."

(Matthew 6:19-21)

One evening during this seven-day sale period, we were headed up to Altoona to a baseball game at the Curve and we stopped at a Giant Eagle along the way, but alas, no gummies. The next day, the last day of the sale, we headed to Greensburg, stopping at the Ligonier and Latrobe Giant

Eagles...no gummies. There are two more stores along Route 30 in Greensburg. We found three bottles at one store and four at the other! We had hit the mother lode! We had found the treasure! Adding those to the three online bottles we had at home, it gave us enough to last over half a year!

You may be thinking...so much time and energy spent and so much excitement over something so silly...And I may tend to agree with you. However, think about it this way: if we can devote our time, energy, and money into something as silly as fiber gummies, and get excited to the point that it's like finding a treasure, how much more excited should we be over finding the treasure that is Jesus Christ! How much time and energy are we willing to spend in getting to know Him better and how excited are we to go on that treasure hunt with other people who need to know Him as well?

"Do not store up for yourselves treasures on earth...but store up for yourselves treasure in heaven...for where your treasure is, there your heart will be also." (Matthew 6:19-21)

The Least of These

Whenever we go to Pittsburgh to a baseball game, we like to walk across the Roberto Clemente Bridge. They close it to traffic before and after a game and it's become part of our tradition. As we're walking, we pass people selling everything from T-shirts and ball caps to water and peanuts as well as people buying and selling tickets...and then there's the people who appear to be homeless. Some of these people play music, hoping passersby will put some money in their instrument cases and some just openly beg for help. We have many terms to describe these people: down on their luck, under-achievers, downtrodden, overlooked...or, as Jesus put it...the least of these.

Jesus had a special place in His heart for the "least of these" ...He chose common fishermen to spread the Gospel, He ate with tax collectors, He gave living water to the woman at the well when no one else would even speak to her. God loves to lift up the lowly. Abraham doubted that God could give him a son and he lied about Sarah being his wife, yet through him, God made the great nation of Israel. Jacob deceived his father, cheating his brother out of his birthright, yet it was his son, Joseph, who saved the nation of Israel from starvation. Moses was a murderer, yet God used him to lead His people out of Egypt, from a life of slavery to the land promised to Abraham. Rahab was a foreigner and a prostitute, yet she has a place in the ancestral line of the Messiah. David was an adulterer and a murderer, yet he is known, to this day, as a "man after God's own heart". Paul was no better than Hitler, but he made many missionary journeys and wrote most of our New Testament.

God used them, with all their imperfections, to bring His plan to fruition...the plan of salvation that He started before the moment of the first sin...the plan that involved some lowly shepherds, a young girl, a common carpenter and a manger in the small town of Bethlehem...the plan that is still in process today, until Jesus returns.

As Christmas approaches, may we be counted among the "least of these" and may God use us to spread the Gospel to our family and friends, to our neighbors and co-workers...to the rest of the "least of these". And if we see someone in need, begging for help, may we be Christ to them, because Jesus said in Matthew 25 that when we do something for the "least of these", we do it for Him.

Letters

Caitlin recently returned from touring with the Continentals (a missionary group that uses song and choreography to bring the Gospel to people all over the world). While she was away, she was unable to use her cell phone (not sure why...maybe so the kids could focus on the ministry) and she rarely had access to a computer. She was on the Pacific coast, so with the three-hour time difference and her schedule, it was difficult to find a good time to call. We wanted to be able to encourage her and, therefore, had to rely on sending letters. I used to write letters all the time...now, I rarely do. When I want to talk to someone, it's just easier to pick up the phone...or send an E-mail. We received one letter from Caitlin...which I will cherish considering the day and age in which we live. We are fast approaching a time when hand-written letters will be all but obsolete! How interesting it was to see her handwriting and to know her thoughts. Yes, this letter will be tucked away with some of the other special things I've saved over the years...love letters from my husband, cute pictures that the kids made, and other letters from friends and loved ones...some of them gone. Sometimes I get into that special place to look at these treasures, thus keeping the memories alive.

I am currently reading a novel entitled "Silenced," part of a trilogy by Jerry Jenkins. It takes place in the future...at a time when all religion is outlawed and religious books, for the most part, have been destroyed. The Christians of the day have to meet in secret, knowing that if they are caught, they will be killed. They cherish the Bible, God's Word, or letters to them and they have copies tucked away so that they can get them out and read them, thus keeping their faith alive.

Many of our friends and relatives have cell phones from the same company and, therefore, we enjoy free "in-network" calling. (We have five in our house!) We also can E-mail just about everyone we know...although there are a few of you lurking out there without those capabilities...and you know who you are! We take for granted being able to keep in touch...it's just so easy! We also live in a country where we enjoy freedom of religion. We can go to church as often as we want and own as many Bibles as we please. (I can't even count how many we have!) We many times take for granted that freedom...skipping church because of other obligations or because the rest of the week was so hectic that Sunday is a good time to sleep in and "do brunch." We have Bibles that rarely get read...but they look nice on the coffee table!

We had to work hard to keep in touch with Caitlin... sending things ahead of time, judging how long it would take to reach her, knowing that she was on the move the whole time and it made me realize how blessed we are to be able to keep in touch so easily with those we love.

We had to work hard to keep in touch with Caitlin... sending things ahead of time, judging how long it would take to reach her, knowing that she was on the move the whole time and it made me realize how blessed we are to be able to keep in touch so easily with those we love. The characters and events in the book I'm reading are fictional, but it causes me to wonder how our faith would hold up under such persecution. In order to grow in our faith, we have to cherish God's Word, just like I cherish Caitlin's letter. We need to take it out, read it, and apply it to our lives. We have to work hard to keep from being swallowed up by the ways of the world. We need to spend time worshipping God and fellowshipping with other believers. We need to <u>not</u> take for granted our faith! How interesting it is to read God's letter to us and to know His thoughts.

Well, you can tell that I live with a preacher! Just as a side note...I think I'm going to write letters to my children so that they can put them in their own special places and get them out from time to time...see my handwriting...know my thoughts.

Changes

We took Charlie back to college at the end of August and I marveled at the things he took in comparison to what I took. Much of it was the same, but there were two things in particular that were very different: my portable electric typewriter vs. his laptop and printer and the record player my sister got for her 16th birthday and had passed down to me eight years earlier vs. the "state of the art" stereo with a 51 CD capacity! Changes!

The other day, my Mom called and as we were talking, she mentioned that she found some old children's records and wanted to know if we had something on which Caleb could play them. I told her that it depended on how old they were and, therefore, what speed they were. The record player he has (that was Charlie's) can play 33's and 45's but not 78's. I realize that anyone in their mid-20's or younger most likely has no idea what I'm talking about! Records played at a speed of 78 rpm's were pretty much a thing of the past when I was a child in the 60's, so by the time this record player was purchased in the 80's, that speed was no longer an option. Of course, these records were 78's and so I told Mom that we wouldn't be able to use them but that she should hang onto them for the sake of nostalgia. Changes!

We recently spent time with some friends who have a vehicle that constantly updates you on the temperature outside and has a feature where the headlights come on automatically when the vehicle "decides" that it has gotten dark enough to need them. They also have a device in their boat that not only tells you the depth of the water as you troll along, but whether or not there are any fish to catch. Changes!

Life is full of changes...some good, some bad. Many of the changes we face are good ones. When you make a mistake on the computer, you can go back and fix it without starting all over again. CD's have a better sound than records ever could and are less likely to scratch, warp or skip. I'm not much for fishing, but it seems to me that knowing where they are sure beats trying to find out where they are on your own.

This month, we are facing the 1st anniversary of September 11, 2001...a day of incredibly heart-wrenching changes. When the changes come that are hard to accept, it is good to remember what Paul says in Romans 8:28: "*And we know that in all things God works for the good of those who love Him, who have been called according to His purpose.*" We can also read in Malachi 3:6: "*I, the Lord, do not change.*" And in Hebrews 13:8: "*Jesus Christ is the same yesterday and today and forever.*"

In this ever-changing world of ours, we need to remember to thank God for the good changes that come our way. Also, it is comforting to know that we serve a sovereign God who consistently has our best interests in mind and can help us to find the good that comes out of the inevitable bad that occurs in this world.

As you go through the many changes that occur in your life, make sure to take God with you as you go!

Travel Highlights

One of my favorite things to do is to go places where I've never been and see things I've never seen. It can be something amazing...like the Grand Canyon or something as simple as a pretty tree-lined road. Recently, we got to do just that! We made the long trek to Oklahoma and along the way we visited some wonderful places. We were able to see some quaint old covered bridges...the oldest dating back to 1856 and the longest spanning 315 feet! They were very picturesque nestled among the surrounding trees and streams. We also got to go up in the Gateway Arch in St. Louis...an impressive architectural feat soaring 630 feet above the Mississippi River! Some of the things that we saw were man-made and some were part of nature's beauty...but I could see God's hand in them all!

Even though I thoroughly enjoyed seeing all of these things, the highlight of the trip was seeing a little girl...Emily Anne...our new-born granddaughter! Proverbs 17:6 says that your children's children are a crown and a blessing! I feel truly blessed to live in such a beautiful country and also to have this new little one in our lives!

I Remember a Man

I remember a man who rarely missed church, read his Bible every day and knew the value of prayer. He was a Faithful man.

I remember a man who never tired of reading a story to his grandchildren, even when it was for the tenth time (and he never skipped). He was an Attentive man.

I remember a man patiently showing me how to drive our tractor – it was a "stick." He was a Teacher.

I remember a man who spent countless hours working at his church. He was a Helpful man.

I remember a man who told me that whatever my job, I should do it to the very best of my ability. He was an Earnest man.

I remember a man whose hope was in the Lord. He was a Reverent man.

In Isaiah 40:31, it says that *"those who hope in the Lord will renew their strength. They will soar on wings like eagles; they will run and not grow weary; they will walk and not be faint."*

This same man spent his last few weeks of life in bed. He could not run nor could he walk and his strength was all but gone, but his spirit soared on wings like eagles! He was my **FATHER** and I shall miss him very much.

I Love you, Dad.

In memory of my Dad, Bill Brown

October 21, 1922 -January 12, 1996

Dominoes

D id you ever play dominoes as a child? Remember how simple the rules were: match another player's dominoes and the first player to use up all his dominoes wins! As we grow older, we usually cease to play such childish games, neither having the time nor the desire to do so. Let me share with you an illustration I recently heard which suggests that we should consider playing this game again.

In the game of dominoes, we are to match another player's pieces in the hope of using all of our pieces up. As Christians, we are called to match or meet one another's needs. In 1 Thessalonians 5:11, we read that we are to *"encourage one another and build each other up"*. In Romans 12:15, we read that we are to *"rejoice with those who rejoice and mourn with those who mourn"*. Also in Romans 12:6, we read that we all have been given different gifts which we are to share with one another. As in dominoes, when someone is hurting, we are to "match" them and hurt with them. Likewise, when someone has something good to rejoice about, we should rejoice with them. God has given us many gifts and it's only when we use them all up that we win the game!

So, go find a friend and play a game of dominoes. Encourage one another and everybody wins!

Happy Anniversary!

Well, June is special to us for another reason: it's the month when we celebrate our anniversary. This year will be our 16th! Let me share with you a few things about the man I married and the father of my children.

First and foremost, Chuck is a man after God's own heart. He loves the kids and me very much but he loves the Lord most...and that's as it should be. I wouldn't have it any other way because by loving God first, Chuck is able to love us far better than he could on his own. He's free to love us with the love of God. Let me illustrate.

Last February, Chuck went to a Promise Keepers gathering for pastors down in Atlanta over Valentine's Day. Now, those of you who know me know that I like to make a big deal out of those small days and I was sad to know that my valentine wouldn't be here with me. When that special day arrived, so did a dozen red roses: a very extravagant gift! As much as I loved and appreciated those roses, what touched me even more were the notes I received each day in the mail. He's written them ahead of time and had someone mail them to me each day. That's thoughtfulness.

Most of you also know that I do most of the cooking for the family (and for the most part, we're better off that way!) but, on occasion, Chuck has been known to make dinner in order to surprise me or just to give me a break. Even though I could probably make it better myself, I recognize this as a true expression of his love for me because it isn't one of his strengths and he doesn't even pretend to like doing it! That's sacrifice.

Both of these are examples of what love is all about: putting someone else's interests before your own. Both of these are examples of how Jesus loves us and wants us to love others. Although these gestures were aimed particularly at me, they spilled over onto the kids as well. By Chuck's example, Charlie is learning how to show love to a wife and Carrie and Caitlin are seeing qualities that they should be looking for in a husband. Granted, they won't need this knowledge for quite a few years but you can't wait until they're ready to walk down the aisle to show them what to look for in a mate. Proverbs 22:6 says to "Train up a child in the way he should go and when he is old, he will not depart from it." Chuck and I feel that this training begins even before the child is born. Praying for your children and setting good, Christ-like examples starts long before they can understand your words.

We also read in the Bible where Jesus said to "Let the little children come…" and Chuck has always tried to make time in his busy schedule to spend time with the kids: from "this little piggy" to piggy-back rides; from "wrestle-mania" in the living room to airplane rides into bed; from games of Candy Land to games of run-down in the back yard.

The kids and I have been blessed with a godly man who shows us Christ by the way that he lives his life. Happy Anniversary, Honey! Happy Father's Day, Dad! We love you!

Another Dreary Day

It was another dreary day! Thankfully, I had some baking to do (which I enjoy) and a good book to read...all in preparation for Christmas. Having things to do that you enjoy can make even the dreariest day seem bright...especially when you have something to look forward to. As I'm writing this, there are still nine days until Christmas...I know this because Caleb informs me every morning as to how many days, hours, and minutes we have left to wait! So, I have a lot to look forward to: I need to finish up my baking, decorate the tree (the rest of the house is done), wrap all of the gifts (it's all a matter of having a positive attitude!) and most of all, getting to spend some quality time with my whole family! However, by the time you read this, Christmas will be just another memory...hopefully, a fond one!

...each day of this new year, pray that God will use us to bless someone else.

Just because Christmas is over, it doesn't mean that we don't have anything to look forward to. Think about it...it's a brand-new year with brand new possibilities and brand-new blessings that God is waiting to pour out on us as we continue to put our trust in Him. Maybe we have to wait a long time for something big to happen...like a vacation that we're planning to take or a family reunion or even next Christmas, but there are lots of other things that we can plan to do...each and every day. Quite often, if I happen to be talking to Caitlin before she goes to work (she's a server at a Cheesecake Factory), I tell her to make sure that she's a blessing to the people that she serves. That's something that we all can do...as we start each day of this new year, pray that God will use us to bless someone else. It might be that we send them a card or give them a phone call. Maybe we can pay someone a visit, hold open a door or even just give them a friendly smile.

We definitely have a lot of dreary days ahead in the next few months, but if we focus on how God can use us to be a blessing to others, I'm sure those dreary days will seem a little brighter...and we'll be amazed at the blessings that God pours out on us in return!

Replanting Bulbs

When one of our former churches decided to pave the parking lot, they also paved the alley that went between the church and the parsonage. In so doing, they eliminated a flower bed that ran alongside our garage...a place where we not only planted annuals, but which also contained various kinds of bulbs. We dug up all the bulbs and re-planted them...or so we thought! That next spring, much to our surprise, there were Iris leaves pushing their way up through the pavement! Isn't that amazing? It doesn't seem like something as tender and fragile as a new leaf could make its way through the tough, black surface, but there they were, looking as fresh and green as springtime.

God is so awesome! When the pavement of life has closed over us and we feel like life as we know it is over, God gives us a sign, letting us know that life goes on and He is in control. He gives us the strength to push our way up through all of the trials we face here on earth. And when our life here is done, if we've put our faith in Christ, even death can't stop us from springing forth with new life: just like those Iris leaves!

If You Died Tonight

I 'll be the first to admit that I don't have it all together! I could be more organized and I could keep the house cleaner. I could spend my time more efficiently and I could spend more time reading God's Word. My prayer life can be haphazard and I could be looking for more ways to serve. I could spend more time writing letters to my Mom and less time on Facebook! There! I've said it! I am not a perfect person...not even close! However, I can also say this about myself...I don't have to be perfect because I've been redeemed by the One who is...Jesus Christ...and instead of going on to explain that myself, I'm going to use the lyrics to a song by the contemporary Christian group, Big Daddy Weave.

I don't have it all together. Sometimes I find myself asking 'why oh why.' But I know we don't have forever, so I'd be a fool to let this moment pass us by. So, at the risk of sounding crazy, let me ask you...

If you died tonight, where would you be? Where would your soul spend eternity? Jesus gave His life, if you'd just believe...it changes everything, if you died tonight.

You can call me narrow-minded, but I believe that in your heart there lies the proof. And if you look down deep you'll find it, an empty place that is pointing to the Truth. You can hear His voice inside you, gently asking...

If you died tonight, where would you be? Where would your soul spend eternity? Jesus gave His life, if you'd just believe...it changes everything, if you died tonight.

Say, "I need You...I can't live without You...come and fill my life with Your glory, God."

That's all there is to it. Take some time to think about where you'll be when you die. God has put a sense of Himself in each heart (Ecclesiastes 3:11) and we each need to respond to that sense. We need to admit that we don't have it all together (our sinful nature) and recognize our need for a Savior. We need to call on Him and be saved. (Romans 10:13) Never has something been so simple, yet so eternally important!

Yeah, I definitely don't have it all together...but I know that if I died tonight, I'd be in the Presence of God...would you?

The Birth Sampler

Back in the '80's, when I gave birth to Charlie, Carrie & Caitlin, I made them each a birth sampler to hang in their rooms. Birth samplers are made with some form of needlework depicting homey pictures as well as pertinent information about the baby, such as name, date of birth and weight. They may also include length and time of birth.

When Caleb came along in 1999, I purchased a very ambitious baby sampler and began it. However, taking care of a family of six often got in the way of working on it...not to mention that I was very busy making other kinds of crafts, which I sold at craft shows to earn Christmas money.

We moved into our current home in 2007. The three older kids were grown and so I hung their baby samplers in our upstairs hallway underneath their baby pictures. Caleb had a picture, but still no sampler. I would pull it out periodically and work on it, never feeling satisfied that I had accomplished much because the project was so large and involved.

Fast forward to 2015. We are celebrating Caleb's 16th birthday in January...and I'm feeling guilty over his unfinished baby sampler, hoping I get it done as a keepsake someday before I die! I decided to evaluate and re-adjust my goal. I find a sampler that is much more "doable" and I purchase it. I work on it when Caleb isn't around and finish it on May 17th! He may be too old to have it hanging in his room...but it's not too late to hang it in the hall with all the others!

Is there anything that you've been putting off? Something you've meant to do for years and just can't seem to get it done? Maybe you just need to make up your mind to get it done or maybe you need to evaluate and possibly re-adjust your goal. Some things that we set out to do in life are really important...others...not so much.

There is one thing that all of us need to make sure we do...have a relationship with Jesus Christ. It's the most important thing on our "to-do" list and we definitely need to make sure that we get it done before we die!

TLC

Recently, I burned my finger. It wasn't a bad burn; in fact, it was quite small. However, in spite of its size, it demanded all of my attention! It will never cease to amaze me how something so small can hurt so much! Although I was able to continue on with my daily routine, this little burn consumed my thoughts.

Now, this burn was caused by an iron, and even though it was minor, I was careful not to irritate it. Even such a small burn, if not given proper attention, can become infected, making the problem much worse.

We read in James 3:6 that the tongue is like a fire. We all know that fire can be used for very good purposes, such as giving us warm cooked food for nourishment. Do we also know that, if used carelessly, fire can cause great damage? Verse 5 of James 3 says, "Consider what great forest is set on fire by a small spark."

How do we use our tongues? Are they being used for good purposes, such as warming hearts, nurturing souls, and refining relationships? Or are we starting forest fires all around town? Maybe what we say seems very minor but it will never cease to amaze me how something so small can hurt so much! Remember even a small burn, when left unattended, can grow into something much worse.

By the way, after a few days of "Tender Loving Care," my burn was healed. How about those hearts and souls and relationships? Are they in need of a little "TLC?"

Go Against the Flow

Throughout Jesus' ministry, He was constantly doing things in contradiction to the norm, "go against the flow," so to speak. There was the time that He stayed in the Temple when all the other children stuck close to their parents and the time that He rebuked the moneychangers in the Temple, overturning their tables. There was the time when He and His disciples picked some food out of a field on the Sabbath, when no work was to be done; and there were those He forgave who were shunned by all others.

Jesus lived His life on a different plane, heading in a different direction. He was setting an example for us, a way in which we should live our lives.

As Christians living in a society where the "norm" or the "flow" of life leads to death, we need to make sure that we are, like Jesus, "going against the flow," heading toward the Light, toward eternal life with Him.

Any "wimp" can drift along with the current. It takes strength, moral and spiritual strength, to swim upstream, standing up for what we believe.

So, let's stand firm in our faith and be proud of Jesus and thankful that He's in our lives. And, as people drift by, let's not neglect to share this great joy with them so that their lives can be turned around as well and, together, we can head toward the Light!

Life and a Straight Line

I've always liked math and one of the cardinal rules of math is the fact that the shortest distance between two points is a straight line.

I also like to take trips. Did you know that if you go to New Stanton, Pa and pick up I-70, you can travel to...

*Columbus, Ohio

*Indianapolis, IN

*St. Louis, MO

*Kansas City, MO

*Denver, CO...and beyond

...all on the same road...all in a straight line. It might be the shortest and fastest way to get to where you're going, but it's probably not the most interesting. Many times, when we're taking a road trip, it's much more interesting to detour onto little side roads and see some of the amazing "out of the way" places that are out there.

We, many times, would like our life to be in a straight line...

*We grow up going to school

* We graduate from the college of our choice

* We land a job and get married

* We buy a house, filling it with children that we raise to "perfection"

* We have enough money to enjoy our empty nest and retirement

...but life isn't always like that. We take many detours along the way...some planned, some not, but no matter the path our life takes, no matter how many curves and unknowns we face, we need to always remember that God is in control and that He has a plan for us.

Two of my favorite verses are from Proverbs 3:5-6: "*Trust in the Lord with all your heart and lean not on your own understanding. In all your ways acknowledge Him and He will make your paths straight.*" They might not be straight in the math sense of the word, but you can be sure that your path will lead straight to Him...and He will probably take you on some interesting side trips and show you amazing "out of the way" things!

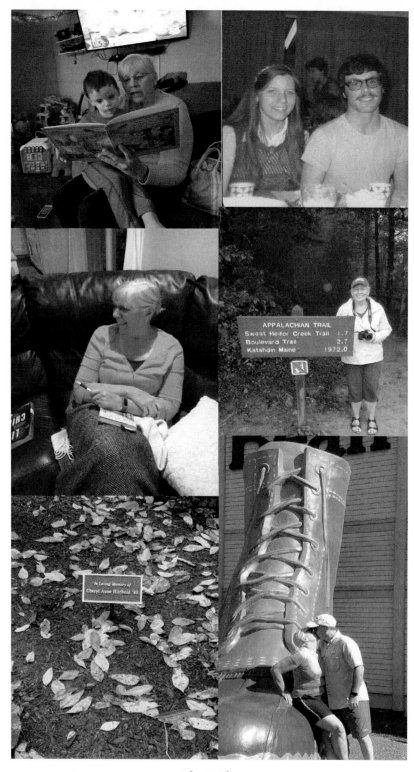

A Little Tinge of Red

I saw something the other day that made me both sad and happy. One of the trees in our yard had just the slightest tinge of red in the leaves. The sad part is, summer is coming to an end. The happy part is, soon the trees will be arrayed in a variety of beautiful fall colors!

I'm sad because I'll eventually have to be putting my sandals away. I'm happy because I'll be able to wear the fun scarf that I crocheted last year to go with my favorite blue hoodie!

I'm sad that because of the two surgeries this summer, combined with an enormous amount of rain, we haven't been able to go biking yet this season. I'm happy because autumn is a beautiful time to go biking and we will hopefully be able to hit the trail several times before it snows!

I'm happy that my life is grounded in my Savior's love and that I'm saved by His grace!

I'm sad because Caleb has already gone back to college. I'm happy because we will see him several times this fall when we go up to watch him in the marching band at the football games!

Life is like that...full of happy/sad moments. As I look at myself in the mirror, I see a much older person than I used to be and I realize that I'm much closer to the end of my life than I am to the beginning...and that makes me a little sad. But I'm happy that my life is grounded in my Savior's love and that I'm saved by His grace...and that I know when the end of my life comes, I'll be with Him!

Imagine...all this pondering from a little tinge of red in the leaves!

Sudoku

Winter is a good time for doing puzzles. I enjoy a good jigsaw puzzle...but only ones that are special to me. For instance, we've been to Washington D.C. a lot, so when we did a puzzle of D.C., it was very meaningful. I also did one with my Mom of the Finger Lakes Region in New York...because that's where we're from. Next up on our agenda is one depicting the National Parks...can't wait! If I can do one jigsaw a year, I'm happy, but on a daily basis, I enjoy doing the Sudoku puzzles that come in the newspaper. Now, don't laugh (like my husband did) when I say that Sudoku can be an exciting and even spiritual thing to do! (It's all in the attitude!)

For those of you who don't know, Sudoku is a square, containing 9 squares with each of those containing 9 squares (81 squares in all). The puzzle makers always start you off with a few of the squares filled in with numbers and the puzzle-solvers job is to fill in the rest. Using the digits 1-9, each row, column, and square of 9 has to contain each digit with no repeats. There are different levels of Sudoku: Easy, Intermediate and Advanced. Once you get the hang of it, the easy ones are so simple that they *lull* you into having the mindset that Sudoku is a "piece of cake."

As you move into the Intermediate level, it gets a bit harder and I usually have to write down possibilities of numbers in each square and then solve by process of elimination. You have to look for clues and use your senses of logic and reason. Many times, it can look hopeless and then you find "that one clue" that unlocks the whole puzzle. More than likely, it was right under your nose the whole time...you just had to see it from the proper perspective. Sometimes, I put the puzzle aside for a while and then come back to it later...seeing it with "fresh eyes" can make all the difference. Occasionally, you'll solve a section of the puzzle with ease, but then get stuck on the others. It's also possible to make a wrong move (you realize this when you find that you've repeated a particular number in a row, column or square) and at that point, you have two options: quit or go back to what you know is right and re-work the puzzle from there. Doing Sudoku not only exercises your brain, it teaches you perseverance and patience as well!

Ultimately, completing a Sudoku puzzle comes down to trusting the puzzle-maker that there is, in fact, a solution and then sticking it out until the end...at which time you can feel satisfied in your accomplishment and know that you did the job well.

I hope through all of this that you can see a correlation here between Sudoku and life...and our relationship with God. Life starts out easy and gets a whole lot more complicated. God has given us the clues to solving the puzzle of life in His Word, but we need to use our reason and logic to understand them.

Sometimes we just need to see things from the proper perspective...through God's eyes! Sometimes we think that life is a "piece of cake" and we try to solve it on our own, only to find that we've made a mistake. God doesn't want us to quit, He wants us to persevere and to finish the race (see Acts 20:24) so that He can say, "*Well done, good and faithful servant.*" (see Matthew 25:21).

Ultimately, we need to trust in our Maker that life has a purpose and follow His clues to find our purpose in Him.

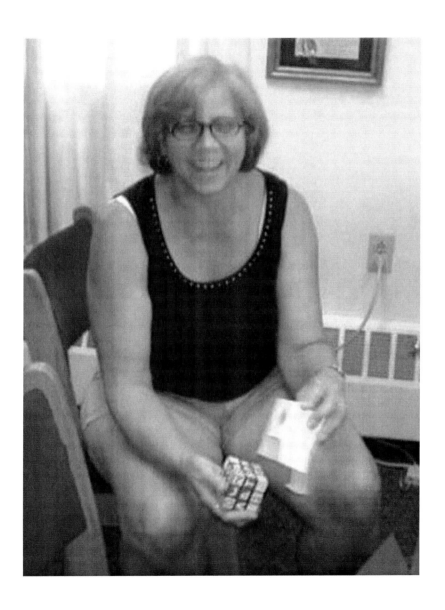

As a Parent

As a parent, I love planning fun things to do with the family...whether it involves something as big as taking a trip or something as small as a surprise movie or even a game night! When the kids were younger, we didn't take too many trips, but when we did, it was always a surprise to them. We usually didn't tell them too much about where we were going...just enough to pique their interest. They simply trusted us and went along for the ride...expecting something wonderful even when they didn't know what to expect! Fridays were always "Family Night" at our house. While the kids were in school, I would bake a special treat and get out the games, making sure to run the sweeper so that it would be clean to sit on the floor.

As a parent, making the plans are fun, but the best part comes as I watch the kids enjoying those plans unfold! Of course, the scenario sometimes takes a different turn, for instance, when someone complains about having to spend too much time in the car or they build up a destination in their minds so much that when they discover the reality, it is disappointing. Also, as the kids got older, they would have a tendency to ask too many questions and maybe even try to get in on the planning...which would make things complicated. There were also times when we couldn't agree on which game to play or movie to watch, but overall, I think we've created some great memories.

As a parent, God, our heavenly Father, loves making plans for us...sometimes they are big plans and sometimes they are small, but they are always a surprise and as His children, we need to trust Him and go along for the ride.

In Jeremiah 29:11, God promises that He knows the plans He has for us...plans for a hope and a future, and I'm sure that He delights in watching our joy as those plans unfold. When we interfere with God's plans by asking too many questions or complaining or making plans ourselves, the scenario can change and not be as wonderful as God originally designed. We need to put our lives in God's hands...expecting something wonderful even when we don't know what to expect!

The Cubby Hole

We have this wonderful "cubby hole" in our closet. Actually, it's more than a cubby hole because I can climb up into it and actually stand up. It's a terrific storage place year-round, but at this time of year, it's a great hiding place for Christmas gifts.

Now, I'm not letting the cat out of the bag because the kids know for a fact that this is where their gifts are. We've already discussed this with them and told them that if they don't want to be surprised on Christmas morning, to go ahead and look! Of course, we're hoping that they'll want to be surprised and that they'll wait until the appropriate time. For you see, it's in that time of waiting where hopes and dreams are made. Part of what makes Christmas so special is the expectation and anticipation!

I think back to many years ago when Mary and Joseph and many others were waiting for the appointed time...all of their hopes and dreams building in the expectation and anticipation of God's greatest Christmas gift...His Son, Jesus. I think of the shepherds who made their way to yet another "cubby hole," seeking their gift, their Savior!

Yes, part of what makes Christmas special is the waiting and sometimes, when the waiting is over, we're thrilled with the gifts we've given and received and sometimes, we're not. But the greatest gift we can receive (and give) on Christmas is the love of God and knowledge that we can have salvation through His Son, Jesus. And this, my friends, is the gift that never disappoints!

Hearers and Doers

How often do you find that you've been listening to someone, but haven't really heard? Maybe you hear the music, but don't pay attention to the words or maybe you sit through a sermon or a class at school, but once home, you can't recall what was said?

If this has happened to you, you're in good company because this has happened to all of us at one time or another. But don't find too much comfort in this company because this is something against which we need to guard ourselves.

James 1:22 tells us that we must *be doers of the Word, not hearers only,* lest we be deceived. In Romans 2:13, we read that *those who hear the Word are righteous in God's sight,* but it is those who obey it who will be declared righteous in the end.

So, as Christians, we need to make sure, first, that we are hearers of the Word: reading the Bible, listening to the sermon, etc., <u>and</u> that we are putting it into practice by living Godly lives and proclaiming His Word to others. Let's make sure that we are hearers and doers of the Word.

Not Really an Option

I t's "Back to School" time already! Where did the summer go? Going back to school can be a busy, hectic time of getting ready...there are new clothes to buy in addition to school supplies, backpacks, shoes and lunchboxes; there are quite possibly annual physicals or sports checkups and trips to the dentist and eye doctor; there are earlier bedtimes and waking up times; and then there's the homework...but we do it because it's what's best for our kids and because we don't have an option. I think we can all agree that getting an education is important and beneficial to our children...and so worth the hassle involved!

Getting to church and Sunday School can be a bit of a hectic time as well...there may be new clothes to buy occasionally in addition to shoes and a good Bible; there are earlier bedtimes and waking up times; and then personal and family devotions during the week...but we do it because it's what's best for our family and because we don't have an option...

Well, I wish that we didn't have an option, but we do. Unlike going to school, going to Sunday school and worship is optional. There are no laws requiring you to attend and unfortunately, many people opt to do something else on Sunday mornings...working on a project at home, spending quality family time, participating in sports or just plain sleeping in. People wouldn't think of allowing their children to skip school for any of those reasons...but for some, participating in Sunday School and worship has become the option that is chosen only when there's nothing better to do.

How sad. Parents, we need to show the same commitment to our church that we show to everything else that we do in our lives. We need to be teaching our children the importance of developing our relationship with God...that it's more important than anything else that we do because having a personal relationship with God and being committed to His church can direct our whole lives...not to mention the eternal benefits!

So, as you're preparing to begin the new school year, make plans to be in Sunday school and worship on a regular basis as well. I think we can all agree that spending time in worship and Sunday school is important and beneficial to our children and adults...and so it's worth the hassle involved!

Busy

Busy! Now, there's a word with which we can all identify! I remember a time when we'd say, "When Christmas is over and things settle down..." or "After Easter, when things aren't so busy." Granted, those are still extremely busy times, but things don't ever seem to "settle down" anymore. Every day seems to be filled with an endless list of things to do and places to go. There's no such thing as being "caught up" anymore.

We need to be very careful with these busy lives of ours. Let me give you an example. Last Sunday, Chuck and the three older kids headed off to Sunday school while Caleb and I stayed home. He needed to be fed his cereal and I needed to finish getting ready for worship. As I looked around the house, every floor was dirty and there were piles of mail and books everywhere. Caitlin was to leave for camp after church and she wasn't even packed yet...I had no idea what we were going to have to eat after church either! Needless to say, it was very tempting to want to skip worship and get "caught up." Caleb was tired and could, no doubt be coerced into a nap and I'd be all alone...oh, what I could accomplish in that hour! I had a choice to make: I could either stay home and work or go to church and worship.

This dilemma of whether to work or worship is nothing new. In the book of Luke, Chapter 10, we read of two sisters, Martha and Mary. Jesus came for a visit and Martha was busy tidying up and preparing food while Mary sat at Jesus' feet and listened to what He had to say. Martha complained that Mary wasn't helping, but Jesus told her that Mary had chosen the right path. You see, Jesus knew that if Martha would take the time now to worship Him, that later, everyone could pitch in and take care of what needed to be done.

As Christians, we should keep this story in mind and always choose to worship. The work that we have to do will wait...believe me...it's not going anywhere! But our opportunity to worship on Sunday morning will come and go and if we miss it, then we've missed it forever, for no two worship experiences are the same.

So, I went to worship that Sunday...and my untidy house gleefully met me when I returned home and I was able to face it, knowing that I'd made the right choice!

P.S. When we got home, Caitlin packed and the rest of the family tidied up while I prepared lunch...I definitely made the right choice!

Kindergarten

Kindergarten sure has changed a lot from when I went. I don't remember too much about it except playing with the "life-sized" kitchen (from my perspective), taking naps, and chasing a boy around the room. During the past year, Caleb received two report cards from his teacher. They didn't receive grades, just an "S" for satisfactory or an "N" for needs improvement. The children were evaluated in 30 different areas! I never knew there were that many things to even consider at the age of 5/6. I can proudly say that he received 29 "S's" on each report card. I guess I need to tell you that what he received an "N" in was...tying shoes! Both times! The only time we would think about teaching the process was when we were tying his shoes while he was brushing his teeth as we ran out the door for school. Obviously, that was not a time conducive to either teaching or learning. I don't even remember when or how the other kids learned, but I did tell them that there was $10 in it for whoever taught Caleb how to tie. But, with their own sources of income, $10 was not much of an incentive.

You can bring all your concerns to God.

Now that Kindergarten is over and summer is in full swing, I am pecking away at my summer "to do" list. Let's see, there's the 25th anniversary trip out west-check, Annual Conference-check, Vacation Bible School-check, Mommy and Me Camp-check, our family trip to Baltimore and Rehoboth Beach-check, Caleb learning to tie his shoes-check...yes...while we were down at the beach, all the times he'd watched just clicked and he tied his shoes! We were all so proud...and relieved! Once he was sure that we'd all seen him do this marvelous deed, he proceeded to seek out members of the extended family who were also at the beach to impress them as well. All in all, learning to tie your shoes is a very small part of life, but to Caleb, it was as if he had climbed Mount Everest.

Romans 12:15 says to *"Rejoice with those who rejoice."* We rejoiced with Caleb and you can rejoice for me because...oh yeah, that list...teach Caleb to ride a bike without training wheels, teach Caitlin to drive, get Caleb's chore chart up and running again and help him win the grand prize in the summer reading program at the library...and tell you that you can bring all your concerns to God, big and small and you can thank him for all your victories...mountains as well as shoe tying.

P.S. Caleb has his first loose tooth...another mountain!

Easter Egg Surprise

So, on Easter, my sister-in-law was telling us about their egg coloring experience and as she's relating this story to me, I kept thinking...I wish this had happened to me because it would make a great "Ponderings"! Well, it didn't happen to me, but it's still a great story, so here goes. On Saturday, Sal bought four dozen eggs and boiled three dozen of them for coloring later that day. When it came time to color them, she pulled the cartons out of the fridge and the kids did their thing. On Sunday morning, my niece, Nicole wanted to eat one of the eggs. She chose one of the beautiful works of art and cracked it open. Much to her surprise, the egg was raw. It didn't take long for them to figure out what had happened. When the eggs were taken out of the fridge for coloring, the carton of uncooked eggs was mistakenly included with two of the cartons that had been cooked. The problem: choosing an egg because of its beautiful appearance on the outside does not guarantee that you'll be pleased with what's on the inside!

So, on the day after Easter, we went to the Pittsburgh Pirate home opener. Our seats were in the bleacher section where there is handicapped seating available. Shortly after the game started, a group of people showed up, including a man in a wheelchair and a very pretty young lady who appeared to be taking care of him. She had such a pretty face and I thought, "How wonderful of her to be caring for this man who obviously needed a great deal of attention." As the game progressed, the number of beers this woman consumed was incredible and the foul language spewing out of her mouth was "enough to make a sailor blush"! The problem: admiring someone because of their good looks or even their good deeds does not guarantee that you'll be pleased with what's on the inside!

So, a couple of verses to keep in mind: 1 Samuel 16:7 says, "*Man looks at the outward appearance, but the Lord looks at the heart.*" May we see people through God's eyes and so be able to discern the good (and the bad) that's on the inside. Also, Philippians 4:8 says, "*Whatever is true, whatever is noble, whatever is right, whatever is pure, whatever is lovely, whatever is admirable – if anything is excellent or praiseworthy - think about such things.*" If we put this last verse into practice, God guarantees that what's on the inside will be pleasing!

Tribute to Dizzy

We recently had a death in the family...our betta fish swims no more. A year and a half ago, Carrie's colorguard instructor gave all the senior girls a fish as a gift. Carrie was thrilled...of course, that's how Carrie is about any gift. My first thought was: "How presumptuous to give something which involves such responsibility: We have to remember to feed it and change the water and get someone to 'fish-sit' when we're out of town." We almost didn't have to worry about it because while we were talking with the other colorguards and their parents, Caleb made some sort of physical contact with the fishbowl and as we turned to the sound of breaking glass, we saw the fish flopping around on the floor. After a successful rescue, Carrie named her fish "Dizzy." She was very good about taking care of Dizzy...and then she went away to college. Chuck and I took up the task of feeding and we tried our best to put off the cleaning until a weekend when Carrie was home. Dizzy's life was status quo.

Sometime in January, Caleb said that he wished he had a pet. I told him that we have three pets: a dog, a cat, and a fish. He felt that none of these was really his. He wanted a pet of his own; I didn't want any more pets. When brilliance strikes, it's truly a wonder to behold! I decided to ask Carrie if Caleb could have her fish and she said, "Yes"! Caleb could have a pet of his own and I didn't have to add to the number of pets in our house! So, we got a bigger bowl, a tunnel for the fish to swim through, and a cool blue shark. We were in business...for about a month...then Dizzy succumbed to his fate and we're down to a cat and a dog.

I discovered Dizzy's demise just before we left for Sunday School. Unsure as to how Caleb would take the news, we decided it best to wait until after church to tell him. During church, I wondered if we should tell or just go get a substitute fish before he notices. When he was little (one or two) he had a little stuffed lion "Dandy Lion," but he usually just called him his friend. Unbeknownst to Caleb, we lost Dandy Lion on a trip to the mall. We looked everywhere, retracing our steps, but to no avail. I quickly went to the store where I had purchased Dandy Lion and found another one. To this day, Caleb doesn't realize that his friend is actually a substitute. (That is until he is old enough to read this article!) But then I realized that death is a part of life and what better way to teach him that, than with a fish he'd only had for a month.

As Easter approaches, we come face to face with another death. We can pretend like it never happened: substituting eggs and chocolate bunnies for the real meaning of Easter just like we did with Dandy Lion. Or we can realize that Jesus' death is a part of life: Eternal life. Without Jesus, our substitute, we're lost like the original Dandy Lion or dead (in our sins) like Dizzy.

Have a blessed Easter as we celebrate God's love for us!

Oh, by the way, we told Caleb about Dizzy after church...he said he'd like to get a puppy!

Black and White Stickers

So, you know those little black and white stickers that you put on your vehicle to show the places you've been? I love those! Anyone who's seen our van knows that! However, yesterday, I was outside for an hour carefully removing all of those stickers and transferring them to the outside of a bin where we store our maps and tour books. I needed to do that because today, we traded in our van for a new vehicle (well, new to us anyway!). Now that the 2008's are out, our van was officially 13 years old. It's a Dodge Grand Caravan and we bought it used nine years ago when we were expecting Caleb. Since it's an older model, it only has one sliding door and it looks "boxier" than its newer counterparts. There are some rust spots on it and some areas where the paint is peeling off. Also, last winter, I got in one day and the windshield was frosted over on the <u>inside</u>...I'm guessing a bad seal. But the main reason we traded it in is because the transmission is going bad, so we were afraid to drive it too far. With all of that information, I'm sure you agree that we've made the right decision in trading the van for something newer.

When most people looked at our van, they saw something that's seen better days...but when I looked at our van, I saw past the blemishes and scars...I saw memories. I could step into that van and look back and see four kids sitting there...Charlie and Caleb in the middle and Carrie and Caitlin in the way-back. In addition to removing the stickers, I also made a sweep of the van to clean it out. I found an extra car seat clip for Caleb and the license plate list that Charlie made from 2005. I found a pony-tail holder from one of the girls and the container of band aids we always carried with us...now too old and sticky to use. I even found the hood ornament that mysteriously came up missing from the hood...never did solve that one! I found directions to some of the places we visited and the sun shield we used to put up to keep the sun out of Caleb's eyes. I saw the great CD player that we had installed as a surprise for one of our trips. We would all bring CD's and take turns putting one in...sharing in each other's music...my favorite one being "Auntie Grizelda" by The Monkees...just to irritate the kids! I can hear us playing the alphabet game and "I Spy" and I can still see Charlie bolting from the van when Caleb threw up unexpectedly one night after driving around to look at people's Christmas light displays!

Well, we left our van in good hands...hopefully to be restored so that it can be used to create more memories for another family. The salesman asked me if I was excited about getting a new vehicle...I said that I had mixed emotions. He thought that my reservations were because we were taking on a new financial responsibility, but I said that I was going to miss the van. I think he thought I was crazy, but I was able to look at that van with a fondness and love that no one else could understand...kind of the way that God looks at us. He sees past the blemishes and scars and loves us unconditionally for who we are...and who we can become. In fact, He loves us so much that He sent His Son to be our Savior...Jesus Christ, born a baby in Bethlehem...come to earth to provide a way for man to find his way back to God. You see, if we allow Him to, He restores us back to the way we were created to be...in right relationship with Him.

If you haven't already done so, I pray that you open your heart to Him this Christmas...take that trip to Bethlehem and meet the Baby who can change your life...and if they have any of those little black and white stickers...

The Best of Both Worlds

Remember when the kids were small and you had to dress them and tie their shoes (many times a day) and wipe their noses (and other places on their bodies) and bathe them and cut the crusts off their sandwiches and help them pick up their toys – always reminding them that they were supposed to put some toys away before getting others out? Those days seemed endless and you dreamed of the day when the kids were bigger and could do all of those things for themselves so that life wouldn't be so hectic – right? WRONG!

I am smack in the middle of a summer where my three older children have jobs – all at different times and days. Charlie can drive (which doesn't always help because we sometimes need that vehicle to chauffer the girls to their jobs). Carrie has her permit and needs some quality driving time so she can get her license in the next six months. Caitlin wants her permit, but she needs to have a physical first. Oh, and Caleb needs a physical before he can go to kindergarten, which is rapidly approaching.

Carrie is changing colleges and needs to register. I think I only have to buy one backpack, but three pairs of tennis shoes. From the looks of the laundry, we need to do some serious shopping for undergarments. Three of them need eye appointments, two of which involve contacts and glasses. As far as the dentist goes: two down, two to go!

The list goes on and on...all the while trying to maintain a consistent quiet time as well as time for exercise, family dinners (including anywhere from 3-6 of us depending on the night), quality time with my husband, family and friends and time spent wishing we owned a cow because of the many trips I make to the store for milk. Oh, and stock in General Mills or Kellogg's would be nice too!

Life can drive us crazy! That's why it's so important – essential – to be firmly grounded in Christ. Jesus offers us a *peace that passes all understanding* (Philippians 4:7) – and I need that because some days I can't make sense of my life as it pulls me in so many directions. I do make sure I spend time with God each day and believe it or not, I do it while I'm on the treadmill – thus killing the proverbial two birds with one stone.

Remember when the kids were small and you dreamed of the day when they were bigger...remember Caleb...I'm still cutting the crusts off sandwiches and picking up toys...the best of both worlds!

Garage Possibilities

I was driving down the road a few months ago and noticed that someone was building, what looked to be, a garage...since there was already a house on the property. It was at the stage where there were enough 2x4's to give it a shape and a roof. I'd been through there a few days before and hadn't noticed it being there, so I thought that they had done a fair amount of work in a short time. I remember wondering if they were Amish...

I've never been to an Amish barn-raising, but I've read about them and would love to see one first-hand sometime. From what I understand, the whole community pulls together and gets the job done in a day! For the most part, the men do the building and the women prepare all kinds of food and they make a day of it...the whole body giving of their time and effort to one particular family...the perfect picture of unity!

I used to have all week to get things done around the house, but now that I work part-time, Saturdays seem to be the day for chores. When you're used to having a whole week to do things, trying to fit them all into one day can be frustrating, to say the least...especially when you see other family members enjoying a leisurely day off! I quickly discovered that teamwork was the solution to my dilemma. I assess the situation and write down all the chores that I feel need to be accomplished and put it on the dining room table, telling whoever else is home to pick a job and check it off. When we all work together, the jobs get done quickly...and then we can all enjoy a leisurely day off!

In John 13:34 & 35, Jesus commands us to love one another...so that all people will know that we are His disciples. When we are unified, when we work together, when we love one another...Jesus becomes known to the world!

By the way, I drove past that "garage" again just the other day...it's still just a skeleton of a possibility...maybe they're out of money, maybe they're short on time...or maybe they just need a little help! No matter what it is we're trying to accomplish, it's always better when done with others. At home and at church...be an example of unity...and be an example of Christ!

Carrie's Birthday Letter

Mom, writing this was actually pretty difficult. Not only because of three little children who need me all day but because there are so many things I admire about you...so many ways I aspire to be like you.

I want to start with things I admire about you. Growing up you always made every house feel like a home. I can't say I prefer one house over another because you made each one special. You always made us finish whatever we started. We didn't always like it but it taught us to be faithful in our commitments and to not give up when things get hard. You let me be myself. I was such a tomboy...still am a little. You never tried to change me even though you are nothing like that. You have been and continue to be very generous. Giving of your time and money...not only to your kids but people in your church. I have always loved your "Ponderings." You have such a way with words...like Dad does at the pulpit. You nursed and stayed home with us even when it wasn't a popular thing to do...you put our needs first. Lastly, you live your faith! I've never had to question whether you were saved. Not everyone can say that.

The next part is better as a list:

I love that you and I have similar tastes.

I love that we can crochet together.

I love that you always look so nice.

I like that you dressed Caitlin and me in matching clothes when we were little. I love that you made most of them.

I love sharing recipes with you.

I love your attention to detail whether it's grammar, planning trips, or decorating your house.

I love our shared love of tomato soup. That always made me feel special growing up.

I love that you made Christmas so magical.

In East Brady, I remember:

Making a tent in the backyard with sheets and the clothesline.

Playing baseball.

The siren going off.

Being Tarzan on the playground.

Feeding the ants.

Hurrying to make Caitlin's bed for you.

Putting my hand through the glass door and you singing "Little Bunny Foo Foo."

Seeing the Christmas lights on the hill as we crossed over the bridge after swim lessons.

Lying on the backseat with my head on your lap as you took me to the hospital with croup.

Sled riding in someone's backyard.

Riding bikes in the parking lot.

In Derry:

Watering your plants.

My Dalmatian birthday.

Singing together as a family.

Blanket forts in the car.

Chocolate chip cookies cakes because I didn't like cake.

B-day party complete with a green bubbly pool.

Telling me to stand up for my faith when learning about evolution.

In Herminie:

Easter egg hunts in the backyard.

Making jelly.

Having our own Halloween.

Yelling up and down the laundry chute.

Going to Pirate games.

Open houses.

In Vandergrift:

Christmas tree mishaps.

B-day angel food cakes.

Hunting for our Easter baskets.

Women of Faith with you.

Setting me up with Ben...best advice ever!

Parsonage dinners.

Accepting Ben and treating him like one of your own.

In Jennerstown:

Visiting me at McDonald's (I loved this!)

Helping to give me a beautiful wedding.

You crying on our first Christmas after moving to Oklahoma.

Throwing a baby shower for Emily.

Giving you a grandchild...and then two more!

Always helping out when you come to visit.

Craft shows.

Visiting the Outer Banks.

Driving back to Oklahoma with me.

Sending the kids seasonal cards.

Helping and supporting Emily and me while Ben was deployed.

Most importantly, you've always prayed for me and been there for me. When I was young, I always prayed for the Lord to give me a friend. Little did I know you were there all along! People have come and gone but you have been my most faithful and best friend.

Happy Birthday! I love you!

Carrie Girl

What is a Christian?

"**M**ommy, what's a Christian?" "A follower of Christ, honey...someone who loves Jesus."

"How can we follow Christ when we can't see Him?" "Well, we read the Bible and follow His example. We also can talk to God and He'll tell us how we're supposed to be." "How can we talk to God? We don't know His phone number?" "We talk to God when we pray."

"So, how can we tell if someone's a Christian?" "Well, it's not up to us to judge a person's heart, but Jesus tells us in the Sermon on the Mount that a Christian will be known by his fruit." "You mean like apples and bananas?" "No, like the fruit of the Spirit listed in Galatians. You know: love, joy, peace, patience, kindness, goodness, faithfulness, gentleness, and self-control. Someone who claims to be a follower of Christ should have those qualities. Of course, nobody's perfect. We all sin and make mistakes, but a Christian should turn away from sinful ways and try to be more and more like Jesus every day. Does that help?" "Yes, but how can I be more like Jesus?"

"You know, when I was growing up, I had a best friend named Cyndi. We walked alike, talked alike, we even dressed alike. We did everything together and got to know each other so well that we could even finish each other's sentences. We were alike because we spent time together. That's how we can become more like Jesus: by spending time with Him."

"I can't jump rope or go skating with Jesus, so how can I spend time with Him?" "Well, He's watching over you when you do those things. He's also listening to see if you're playing fairly and treating others as He would. We've talked about some of the ways that you can spend time with Him: reading your Bible and praying. Also, you can go to Sunday school and church, to Bible studies and Youth Fellowship, Vacation Bible School, and the Church picnic. There are lots of ways a person can spend more time with Jesus so that they can get to know Him better and grow to be more like Him."

"What if someone doesn't do these things; does that mean they're not a Christian?" "Well, honey, remember...we're not supposed to judge, but you've got to wonder..."

"And a little child shall lead them..." Please let this "conversation" lead you to Christ.

Firm Foundation

The other day, our daughter Carrie sent us a video on our phones of our granddaughter, Emily reciting her latest Bible verse: "*But the fruit of the Spirit is love, joy, peace, patience, kindness, goodness, faithfulness, gentleness, and self-control. Against such things there is no law.*" (Galatians 5:22 & 23) I could see Daniel watching and waiting patiently for her to be done so that they could go play. This is the 7th verse that she's memorized and she was very intent as she said it...and then she ran off to play! Such is the life of a child...but these verses will stay with her throughout her life and learning them is helping to build a strong foundation for her young faith!

I know this because it has been true of our four children! We are firm believers in the verse: "*Train up a child in the way he should go and when he is old, he will not depart from it.*" (Proverbs 22:6) Everywhere we lived, we had index cards with verses tacked up on a wall. The kids would sit on the floor with their backs to the verses and practice reciting them each night before going to bed...earning bonus stars on their chore charts! We are also firm believers in the verse: "*I have hidden Your Word in my heart that I might not sin against You.*" (Psalm 119:11) We did what we could to provide a strong spiritual foundation for their young faiths. We not only helped and encouraged them to learn Bible verses, but we read them the stories of God and prayed with them and for them. Most important, we led them by example...not that we're perfect...on the contrary, we let them know that we weren't and aren't...hence our need and their need for a Savior! We made sure that they saw us reading our Bibles and praying and of course, we were always in church...and would've been even if Chuck had not been a pastor! Over the years, we were always hoping and praying that we were making a difference in the lives of our children.

Are you training your children up to love the Lord? Are you showing them the importance of reading and studying God's Word, of praying to God and worshiping Him in church? Are you teaching them and leading them by example? Well, you are...but make sure it's the right example that you're setting!

As I watch the video of my granddaughter, I see another dark-haired girl sitting on the floor, reciting verses...ready to run off and play before it's time to go to bed...and I know that a firm foundation was laid because she's teaching the same verses to her daughter now...and I know that we made a difference...and so is Carrie...and so will Emily!

Canada

Recently, some friends of mine went on a vacation to Canada. I didn't catch the name of the place, but the location was 40 miles from Kingston, Ontario. When I heard that, my mind began to race because when I was growing up, my family vacationed in a cabin on a small lake 40 miles from Kingston. I don't think that they went to the same spot, but just the thought of the possibility ushered in a flood of memories. I remember the fresh, crisp mornings and the sound of the loons. I remember the swimming, water skiing, jumping off the cliffs and the pike I caught that was almost as big as I was. (I've got pictures!) I remember the Smiths and the Reeds, two Canadian families who vacationed with us every year. I remember the beautiful sunsets on the lake and the campfires on the beach at night. I even remember the outhouse!

"The Lord is my rock, my fortress and my deliverer; my God is my rock, in whom I take refuge." Psalm 18:2

All of these are wonderful recollections of days gone by (except maybe the outhouse!), but one of my fondest memories is of the rocks down by the lake. They reminded me of a miniature mountain range and I would spend my days leaping from peak to peak. I can't say what kind of rocks they were. Ninth grade Earth Science was a long time ago! However, I remember them being light in color with many colorful specks and glistening spots that I pretended were precious gems. I wonder what those rocks look like now?

Psalm 18:2 says that *"The Lord is my rock, my fortress and my deliverer; my God is my rock, in whom I take refuge."* Hebrews 13:8 says that *"Jesus Christ is the same yesterday and today and forever."* When I think about that lake in Ontario, I realize that things have no doubt changed a lot but I imagine that those rocks have stayed pretty much the same. It's comforting to know that some things never change. It's of eternal comfort to know that Jesus, our rock, and our redeemer, never changes and that He loves us very much.

P.S. It's also comforting to know that they eventually replaced those outhouses with indoor plumbing!

Parsonage Remodel

It's been really interesting to watch the addition to our parsonage being built. Before it even began, all I had to go by were some plans drawn up on paper, and although they were very good, it was difficult for me to envision how big the new rooms would be and what they would look like. Before the building could even begin, the whole area had to be purged of obstructions...things like our pavilion and the big pine tree along with its far-reaching roots. Once the excavating was done, a truckload of stones was laid to form a solid foundation...then the building began. From the laying of the cement blocks for the garage to the shingles on the roof...the house took shape. Then came the windows and siding...making the outside of the addition looking pretty presentable to passersby. Inside, however, was a different story...and still is, as of this writing...exposed plywood, insulation, and fittings for light fixtures and electrical outlets. There have been a lot of messes along the way...inside and out. Even so, I like to walk out there because I can begin to see what is to come...and I can tell it's going to be amazing! If I ever have any questions, I just ask the builder...because he can already see the finished product in his mind's eye.

I'm sure you can see where I'm going with this story. It's not just the story of the addition to our parsonage...it's my story...and it's your story. You see, God has a plan for each of us (Jeremiah 29:11) and He has written it all down on paper (the Bible). When we commit our lives to God, it's like committing to a building project...the plans may be confusing to us and the process may seem like it's just a big mess...but God can see the finished product...the person we are to become...and we're going to be amazing! So, if we have any questions about it...all we need to do is ask God...the author and perfector of our faith...the Builder.

A Flowering Experience

Some of you have seen the flowers that we planted around the Parsonage. This was a big project, first of all because it was "uncharted territory." When you do something for the first time in a new home, there are many decisions to be made: where to plant and what to plant. Second of all, this project was so large because we planted A LOT of flowers! Although there was a lot of work involved, I won't go so far as to call it a chore. It was actually a delight because of the beautiful outcome. I was somewhat surprised, but very happy to see how the kids pitched in and helped voluntarily. They enjoyed getting down in the dirt – making just the right holes for the flowers to go into and they've been great about watering and weeding too.

As I think about our "flowering experience," it reminds me a lot about our "parenting experience." We bought good topsoil and potting soil for our flowers and that is like the good home that we've provided for our children. The water is the care that we've shown – providing for all of their physical needs. The sunshine is the hugs – all the love that has gone into our parent-child relationship. We even put "Miracle Grow" on our plants and that reminds me of our family devotions and all of the prayers that we have said for and with our children.

As we all know, the summer is upon us and it will fly by and already I can see how the flowers have grown. Funny, but I remember bringing those babies home and "planting" them into our family and I can see how they have grown! How time flies!

My Mom

Moms. They do an awful lot of things that get taken for granted. They do an awful lot of things without receiving any thanks or acknowledgement.

I would like to take a moment to acknowledge just a few of the many things that my Mom did for me when I was growing up. I would like her to know that I noticed and that I hopefully did not take her for granted...I would like to thank her!

Before I was even born, my Mom had to wade into our flooded basement to save the crib that she would need for me in a few short months. She always took good care of me...making sure that I was dressed appropriately for whatever weather we had and that I ate EVERY LAST PEA on my plate! She played with us in the snow and held my hand as we walked from store to store downtown as we did our Christmas shopping.

Mom made every holiday and birthday special...from green Jell-O on St. Patrick's Day to elaborate, homemade birthday cakes to thoughtful and creative gifts. In the summer, she would take us swimming and plan special picnic lunches.

In the fall, my brother, sister, and I would usually win a prize at the Community Center Halloween Celebration...wearing costumes designed and handmade by Mom.

As I grew older, she attended numerous choral concerts and swim meets. After I married and began having my own children, she was always there to encourage me as I ventured into unfamiliar territory. She was my own personal cheerleader!

My Mom has moved on to be with the Lord...but I know that she loved me utterly and unconditionally. We shared a love for logic problems and for Christian fiction and for the Lord...and so I know that I'll see her again someday...and I'll thank her again for being the best Mom I could have had!

Love you Mom!

Feel the Nails

How many of you have ever fallen, raise your hand? (How many of you in the privacy of your own home, sitting all by yourself, just raised your hand?) While on vacation this past summer, I fell down a flight of stairs. The short explanation goes something like this: painted steps, rain, 20-year-old flip flops and hands too full to hold the railing. Fortunately, I went down on the side of my thigh and not on my back or tailbone. My leg was bruised from my hip to my knee: one BIG bruise! I thought that I'd have to spend the rest of the summer looking like that, but I was amazed at how fast the bruise faded. By the end of July, the bruise was completely gone on the surface at least. Four and a half months later, I can still feel where the bruise was. If I touch my thigh (and I don't mean hard), there's still a twinge of pain. I sometimes wonder if the pain will ever go away or if I'll always have it as a constant reminder of what happened.

There's a song called "Feel the Nails" that I like to sing around Easter time because that's when we especially focus on Jesus' crucifixion. It questions whether Jesus can still feel the nails when we sin. Do we cause Him pain when we fail to live up to His standards? I honestly don't know if Jesus still experiences any physical pain from the crucifixion, but I'm sure that He experiences emotional and spiritual pain when we sin. In Genesis, chapter 6, we read that when God saw the wickedness of man, He was grieved and His heart was filled with pain.

At this time of year, we try hard to focus on the real meaning of Christmas, which the world makes very challenging indeed. This Christmas, as you're setting up a nativity and re-telling the story of the joyous birth, don't forget that on the horizon, on a distant hill, is the shadow of a cross; a prophetic reminder of what the future holds for this Holy Baby. And, as the New Year begins, don't let our sinful lives be a constant reminder of what Jesus went through on our behalf.

Let there be joy and peace on Earth as we celebrate Jesus' birth and let there be joy in Heaven as Jesus and all the angels celebrate our re-birth!

Rules for Holy Living

2 Corinthians 5:17 says, "*Therefore, if anyone is in Christ, he is a new creation; the old has gone, the new has come.*"

Speaking from personal experience, when I accepted Christ as my Savior, some of the "old me" left immediately, making room for some of the new life in Christ. On the other hand, some of the old ways were harder to get rid of. In fact, even after these many years, there's still some of that old self rattling around, making it hard for me to be the person that God wants me to be.

How do we know which characteristics are to go and which are to stay? How do we know which new qualities to seek and even when we know the changes that need to be made, how do we go about making them? Listening to sermons, attending Bible studies and Sunday School, sharing in small groups, having a personal quiet time, and reading God's Word are all ways in which we can grow spiritually, even becoming the person God wants us to be.

In Colossians chapter 3, Paul gives us some "Rules for Holy Living". Let me share a few of them with you.

1. Set your hearts and minds on things above, not on earthly things.

2. Rid yourselves of sexual immorality, impurity, lust, evil desires, greed, anger, malice, slander, rage, and filthy language.

3. Do not lie to each other.

4. Don't be prejudiced. God loves us all.

5. Clothe yourself with compassion, kindness, humility, gentleness, and patience.

6. Bear with each other and forgive each other.

7. Put on love, which is the perfect bond of unity.

8. Let the peace of Christ dwell in your hearts.

9. Be thankful!

10. Let the Word of Christ dwell in you richly as you teach and admonish one another with all wisdom, and as you sing psalms, hymns, and spiritual songs with gratitude in your hearts to God.

If you are looking to change your life around, give it to Jesus and start living a holy life.

Candles and the Light

We recently celebrated Valentine's Day...a day which we associate with love. I have to tell you about what Caitlin gave me. For Christmas, she received a candle-making kit that she was very excited about because she really likes candles. Usually, when she gets crafts to make, I help her, but with being pregnant and with the arrival of Caleb, we haven't had the opportunity to make any candles.

Wanting to give me a gift for Valentine's Day, but not having the opportunity to go shopping, she made one of her candles and gave it to me. Now this was a very special gift, not only because I, too, like candles, but because of the sacrifice made to give it. She was looking forward to having these candles for herself, but out of her love for me, made a sacrifice by giving up one for my pleasure.

We are in the middle of the season we know as Lent. Lent is a time of preparation, a time of getting ready to receive the most incredible gift we could ever imagine. The gift is that of salvation, offered to us by God. He made the supreme sacrifice by giving His Son to die on a cross for our sins...because He loves us so much.

What do these two stories have in common? Caitlin gave a light to warm the heart of her Mom and God gave His Son, the Light of the world, to save our souls. It's all about love – God's love!

Things We Learned From Mom

Good morning. I wanted to take a minute to show you a side of my Mom that many people didn't see. You may know her as the Pastor's wife, and while she was always the Pastor's wife, whether at home or church, there was another side of Mom that many of you probably didn't have the privilege to see as much as we did. As any of you that are parents can attest to, one of the biggest responsibilities of being a parent is teaching your children, and with that in mind there are a few things I wanted to share with you that we learned from our Mom.

-We learned from my Mom that chocolate chip cookie dough has raw eggs in it, and you shouldn't eat it...but if you saw Dad get a spoon then it was time to dig in.

-We learned that everything you do during your day can be enhanced by some really good music.

-We learned that there was a good meal and dessert for every holiday, and that those foods usually have a color that coincides with that holiday.

-We learned that every movie has a "good part" and it's sometimes a lot easier, and a lot more enjoyable, to just skip to the good parts of all your favorite movies.

-We learned that your grammar better be done good, or you'll be corrected.

-And if you corrected that sentence that means she taught you as well.

-We learned that it's perfectly acceptable to ride in the car and "head bang" to Bohemian Rhapsody when it comes on, regardless of who sees you.

-We learned that Christian romance novels aren't dirty, and are quite enjoyable, regardless of how much your oldest son makes fun of them.

-We learned that sleep deprivation leads to the belief that you can fly up the laundry chute, so you don't have to walk up the stairs, but it also gives you the ability to fall asleep in mid-sentence.

-We learned that everything is better when peanut butter is involved.

-We learned that combining banana slices and orange juice isn't just a convenient way to eat fruit, but it was quite good as well.

-We learned that all of the decorations in the house have a specific place to be displayed, but also a specific place to be put away, and there's no way to edit either of those.

-We also learned that the easiest way to drive your mother crazy was to move pictures around.

-We learned that Zion National Park is one of the most beautiful places on the planet.

-We learned that lighthouses and covered bridges are beautiful, especially in their simplicity.

-We learned that you have to steep the iced tea for at least five minutes, or it just won't be strong enough.

-We learned that homemade soup is even better if it's in a bread bowl.

-We learned that there are a TON of Hallmark movies, and they aren't for everyone.

-We learned that the 4th child has it a lot easier than the other 3, and that 9 PM bedtimes apparently don't exist when you're in high school.

-We learned to appreciate the little things in life: a beautiful sunrise or sunset, snow sticking to pine trees and the colors that all of the leaves change to every year.

-We learned that the most special place in the world was Grove City College, particularly Harbison Chapel.

-We learned that finding that one special person to share your life with is the most rewarding experience.

-We learned that the first time you become a parent you become spoiled by how sweet your first born is.

-We also learned that when you add a second child in, they are always the instigator. Always.

-We learned that the third child gives the kids the advantage in the family for the first time, and they should never use that to their advantage.

-We learned that we should always say: Thank You. Yes, Thank you. Uh Huh.

-We learned that the surprise 4th kid was the missing piece to the family you never knew you needed.

-We learned that you should never stop trying to make out with your husband, even if all four of your kids try to get in between the two of you.

-We learned that adding sons and daughters in-law was the exact same as adding additional children, and that they are loved in the exact same way.

-We learned that becoming a grandparent is even better than becoming a parent, and it only gets better the more grandchildren you add.

-We learned to never lose hope and never stop believing what God can do, whether it's a lost engagement diamond, a missing cat, or fighting through a long painful illness.

-We learned that you should be showing God's love to everyone through your actions, and that God can use even the worst of your days for something good.

-We learned that this life is not the end, it's just the beginning.

-We learned that God will chase you down to let you know that you are His.

-And we learned that even on our darkest days, from our deepest pain through it all, our hearts will be choosing to sing praise.

Looking for the Good

Well, we did it! We moved! The movers were four hours late and it was the hottest day of the season. They brought the biggest truck they had and, in the end, had to tie some of our possessions onto the back of the truck! (Really!) It was a fairly organized move with each box and bin marked clearly. Even the bedding had been cleaned and put in separate bags marked as to which room it went.

Even with all the organization, it was a grueling experience. However, nothing was broken and everything has been located, except for a decorative slate I've yet to find. We spent weeks packing and preparing for the move and have spent the weeks since, unpacking and settling our new home. Chuck settled his office and the three older kids each settled their own rooms (mostly) and the task of settling the rest of the house fell to me.

This settling process is a big job...deciding where everything is to go, then, actually putting it there, not to mention redecorating a whole new set of walls. However, it's been a very rewarding process because the house is looking beautiful and feeling more and more like home every day. It's a big, old house, remarkably well kept. The rooms are spacious with high ceilings. We fully use all four floors and the five staircases.

There are two stairways leading up to the first floor from the basement and two leading up from the first floor to the second floor and one leading up to the attic, which is where our room is located. As much as I try to consolidate my trips, I find that I spend a lot of time each day traveling from floor to floor; going up one set of stairs and then going down another, only to hit a third set of stairs on my way to a fourth.

The upside of this is that it's good exercise. The downside is that it's hard to catch up with someone when you want them. One of the kids may spot me on a staircase and then decide that they need to talk to me, but by the time they reach the place where they thought I'd be, I've already taken another set of stairs and am on a totally different floor!

As I mentioned, the house is old and, therefore, solidly built. Trying to call for someone who is on a different floor or in another staircase is done to no avail. So, we spend a lot of time chasing each other around which, at times, can be frustrating, but usually very comical.

All of these experiences have an upside and a downside, a positive side and a negative side. God calls us to look for the good in all situations. In Matthew, Jesus talks about a tree being recognized by its fruit, whether good or bad. He says in 12:35a that, "*The good man brings good things out of the good stored up in him.*" As Christians, we should be growing more like Jesus every day, storing up good in ourselves, so that only good will come out of our lives. People will see that good and recognize Jesus in us and hopefully want that for their lives as well.

By the way, if you'd like to come and visit us and take a tour of the house, park on the street and when you're done, you will have taken 78 steps! (And that can be a good thing!)

Christian Concert

Recently, our family had the privilege of attending a Christian concert. We really enjoyed the music as well as some time spent with friends, but something else, something very special happened that night. The singer took some time to share a little about his relationship with Jesus Christ and went on to say that Jesus desires to have a relationship with each and every one of us. He invited those who wanted a relationship with Christ to come forward and boy did they!

Counselors had been lined up before the concert and rooms set aside in another part of the large church, but so many came forward that the only room large enough to handle that many people was the sanctuary...where the concert was going on. After a time of prayer, the singer stood up and announced that due to the response, the concert had come to an end. He hoped that everyone would understand that so many lives coming to Christ was more important than any songs he could sing.

How true! What in our lives could possibly be more important than Jesus Christ?

In Philippians 2:10-11, we read that, "*at the name of Jesus, every knee shall bow in heaven and on earth and under the earth, and every tongue will confess that Jesus Christ is Lord...*"

Every single person who has ever lived will bow down to Jesus Christ some day and confess Him to be Lord. Those who have lived their lives here on earth for Him will be bowing in adoration and praise, but those who have lived their lives selfishly, with no time for Jesus, will be bowing their heads in shame.

Jesus Christ died on the cross to provide the gift of salvation to each and every one of us, but it is up to each individual to accept that gift of salvation. When the day comes for us to bow down before Him, will you be bowing in adoration and praise or in shame? The choice is yours.

I am far from perfect, but I have accepted that gift of salvation and I'd be honored to share it with you!

Stay at Home Mom

31 years ago, when we were expecting our first child, Chuck and I decided that once the baby came, I would be a stay-at-home Mom. We knew that it would be tight, financially, but we felt that it was worth it!

In the 1950's, when Chuck and I were born, most women were stay-at-home Moms. But in the 1980's, when we were starting our family, that wasn't such a popular choice. In fact, as a stay-at-home Mom, I often felt that many women who were out in the work force looked down upon my choice as being a waste of a college education...and I often found myself wondering the same thing. Peer pressure is a powerful thing. When you feel that other people are questioning your worth, it's easy to begin questioning it too!

When Caitlin, our third and youngest child at the time joined Charlie and Carrie in school, I was often asked what I was going to do with my time. I thought about getting a job, but then I wondered what I would do about sick kids and snow days and Act 80 days and summer vacation. I wondered about getting the kids off the bus and welcoming them home with fresh-baked cookies and milk. I wondered how all the housework would get done and how we would be able to enjoy a home-cooked meal if I was at work all day. Now, I realize that some women have to and even choose to work outside the home and they learn to balance all of these things...and that's great, but it wasn't what I wanted out of life. Even though I had my periods of doubt, I knew that I had made the right choice and I eventually became very comfortable with it...but it took me a while.

Max Lucado writes: "Does your self-esteem need attention? You need only pause at the base of the cross and be reminded of this: The maker of the stars would rather die for you than live without you!" I came across this statement recently and I wished that I had read it 25 years ago when I was struggling with my self-esteem. You see, I spent my time worrying about what other people thought when, as a Christian, I should have been focusing on how important I am to God. He loved me enough to die for me!

I'm glad to see that a lot of women are choosing to be stay-at-home Moms again and I want to commend them for making that choice...choosing to do without the extra money and the things it can buy...choosing to be the #1 influence in their children's lives...it's an awesome responsibility! If you can make it work, I encourage you young mothers to stay home with your children because more important than having your name on some door or desk or on a tag on your shirt...is having your name on the lips of your children! Be encouraged by this and by the fact that there is a God who loves you, a Savior who died for you...and teach it to your children!

Getting Something New

I t's always great to get something new...until you have to make room for it! When Caleb gets new toys (which happens all at once since his birthday is only two weeks after Christmas), we usually have to go through his belongings, deciding what to keep and what to give away. Sometimes, he's not quite ready to get rid of something and so it goes to the attic...waiting up there if he ever wants it back.

We recently got a new computer. We didn't have to make room for it because it just went where the old one had been. However, the old one still works and we thought it'd be nice to have two up and running...so we had to make room for it! We knew that we wanted it to be on the desk in our downstairs guest room, but the desk was too small. We needed to find a place for the small desk in order to use a larger one that we had in the basement. By moving the desks, we had to rearrange some of the contents of the drawers...evaluating those contents as we went along. We found so many papers that we didn't need...old tax forms and checking account statements from accounts that were closed...things that definitely needed to go! However, we also found some treasures...sweet "I love you" notes from the kids and honor roll lists mentioning their names... things that we definitely wanted to keep in a safe place! This was quite a process...but worth it in the end!

Life is like that...putting away childish things in order to make room for the ways of maturity (see 1 Corinthians 13:11) and making room for new members of the family...making room for God in our hearts. When we invite God to come into our lives, *He makes all things new* (see 2

Corinthians 5:17) and, as it always is when we get something new, something old has to go! As we allow God to fill our hearts, He gently lets us know the things that we're to be done with...and they can't just go to the attic like old toys that we may want to play with again...they need to be burned like so many useless papers. But He also points out the treasures that we have in our lives...He lets us see how important they are and helps us to find a safe place to keep them!

May we each evaluate our lives...keeping the good and getting rid of the bad. It'll be quite a process...but so worth it in the end!

Tess & the Umbrella

Spring is still a month away, but we've had some rain lately in this crazy winter of ours, so along with the ice scraper and gloves, we keep an umbrella in the backseat of the car. It was just such an "umbrella kind of day" the other morning when we arrived at work. As I opened up the umbrella, I noticed tiny little holes in it all around the edges. We had only purchased that umbrella last fall when we'd arrived at a Grove City College football game unprepared. I was puzzled by the tiny holes until I thought of a certain little kitty named "Tess" who has a penchant for chewing things. I recalled the day when I had left the opened umbrella down in the basement to dry and I could picture little "Tess" lying beneath this "kitty-sized tent" leaving her mark all around its unsuspecting edges!

An umbrella with holes seems like a likely candidate for the trash; who wants to hold on to damaged and seemingly useless items? This umbrella is indeed damaged, but the fact that the tiny holes are only around the edges makes it far from

God knows that we are damaged....in fact, He knows that we actually started out that way...

being useless. This umbrella is still very capable of fulfilling its purpose...not to mention that it's beautiful: it has purple stripes...my favorite color!

There are many people who possibly feel a lot like this umbrella: damaged and seemingly useless. We start our lives off with so much promise and purpose and then something happens: we find ourselves out of a job or we're diagnosed with cancer and we see no end in sight to the surgeries and treatments and financial hardships, or we maybe find ourselves all alone in the world and we wonder: who wants to keep a damaged and seemingly useless person like me around?

God does! He knows that we are damaged...in fact, He knows that we actually started out that way, yet He loves us unconditionally, He has a purpose for each and every one of us...and He thinks we're really beautiful!

New Mom and Vehicles

As a new Mom (again), I'd forgotten how utterly dependent a child can be. I not only have to feed, change, bathe and entertain Caleb, but I'm also his "vehicle," so to speak, to show him the world. Now that he is able to sit up and hold his own toys, I can see him, ever so slightly, gaining some independence.

Caleb's brother, Charlie, is becoming so independent that soon he will be able to drive on his own. I'm definitely not his "vehicle" anymore.

Watching them become independent, mature adults is often a happy / sad thing to do. We want them to become who they're supposed to be and to do that, we need to be willing to let go, giving them the freedom to do just that.

Knowing how much freedom to give and when to give it is one of the many challenges of being a parent. When Caleb learns to walk, he'll still need guidance: stairs are a dangerous thing, as are streets and many other things in life. Charlie, though almost grown, still needs guidance: streets are also a dangerous thing for him, albeit in a different way.

When we finally do let go, releasing them into the world, we need to make sure that we're also releasing them into God's hands, knowing that only with God as their vehicle, can they truly be free!

Dawning of a New Day

When the kids were little, I used to enjoy rocking them to sleep, listening for when their breathing became even and peaceful. Now that they're bigger, they pretty much put themselves to bed, our job being to see that all the necessary things get done: clothes out for the next day, Bibles read, teeth brushed, a path cleared on their floor (just kidding) and dirty clothes thrown down the chute. We end this whole ritual with a prayer offered up on our knees by the bedside followed by hugs, kisses and "I love you's."

Most evenings, this process runs pretty smoothly and all is well when the kids are tucked under their covers. However, there are some evenings when bedtime can't come soon enough (okay parents, you can stop nodding your agreement now) and between my impatience and their obstinacy, the hugs are rather limp and the "I love you's sound pretty hollow. When this happens, it's very important to let our children know that we love <u>them</u>, but that we don't always like what they say or do. What amazes me is that I can put my kids to bed feeling frustrated with them, yet when I wake them up the next morning, all the frustration is gone. With the dawning of a new day comes a new start.

In Lamentations 3, we read that God's mercy for us never fails and that it is new every morning. In other words, God doesn't hold a grudge. So, no matter what we've done, how we've lived our lives up to this point, God has mercy for all of us. Hallelujah! Isn't that what Easter is all about?

Nana

Memories are an amazing gift from God. With very little effort, we are able to recall so many things from our past...both good and bad...all of which can be used by God to shape us into who we were designed to be. Think about it like this: when we recall a good memory, we can thank God for the beautiful sunrise we saw or the newborn baby we held in our arms. When we recall a painful memory, we can thank God that it caused us to rely more fully on Him and that He carried us through that time.

My mother-in-law, Sally – or "Nana" as we've called her for the past 36 years, passed away this month and many memories have resurfaced as we talked...about old times and with old friends and family...reminiscing while watching a video montage of her life.

Nana was a strong, accomplished woman with a love for family and a sound faith in her Savior. She will be missed, but we have so many wonderful memories to sustain us here on earth...and a forever in Heaven to look forward to...making some new, unimaginable memories in the presence of our Savior!

Airplanes and Storm Clouds

It was raining when we took off from San Antonio. I like to fly, for the most part. I'm not afraid of heights...in fact, I do my best to sit in a window seat so that I can view God's creation from a different perspective...and hopefully, get some nice pictures. Yeah, I do okay when we're flying up there at 37,000 ft...but I'm a little shaky on the take-offs and landings. You see, I've always had a problem with motion sickness...I don't ride roller coasters and I don't do well on roads that go up and down and wind all around...good thing there's none of those in Pennsylvania!! When I was a kid, I used to have to sit in the back seat of the car in between my older brother and sister (the plight of the "baby") and I remember a couple of times when I warned my Dad that I didn't feel well and he waited a little too long to stop the car...

Anyway, when an airplane takes off in the rain, it has to go through the clouds in order to achieve the desired altitude...which, for me, means that an already shaky take-off is compounded by turbulence! That's how it was this day...as we taxied toward the runway, I looked up and all I could see was a grey ceiling of clouds. It was a rough ride and I prayed the whole way. It seemed it was never going to end and then suddenly, we broke through into a world with blue sky and white, fluffy clouds tinged with the pink of an approaching sunrise...breathtaking! I thanked God for the beauty of the deliverance...likening it to the miracle of a new-born baby after the horror of labor and the peace of God's grace after He's brought us through a trial.

In Psalm 34, God promises that He will deliver the righteous from their troubles. In Joshua 1, God promises that He will never leave us nor forsake us. In James 1, God tells us that our trials come to only make us stronger. So, when we're faced with the storm clouds of life, we need to persevere and claim these promises and trust that when we come through into the light, it will be more beautiful than we could ever imagine...breathtaking!

Let's Talk About Boys

L et's talk about boys. Raising children is a hard job...one that never seems to end. Being in the process of raising four children, two boys and two girls, I am of the opinion that boys are the harder of the two to raise. I'm sure that this statement will bring a variety of responses. For some of you, the raising process may be done (if that ever really happens!), and of that group, some of you agree with me and some of you don't. Others may have small children and just be starting this process and are reading this in hopes of a divine revelation on the subject...too much pressure for me! Let me just share some insights...give you some food for thought...let's just talk about boys.

As many of you know, our new parsonage has a third floor, which we made into our bedroom/sewing room. My sewing machine is in front of a window with a view of our street. I consider my sewing chair to be either a perch or a throne, depending on my mood at the time. One day as I sat on my throne, I watched as some of the neighborhood children walked home from school. The smaller children are safely escorted home by some form of caregiver, while the 4th, 5th and 6th graders walk home on their own. They form the usual groups. You have your pockets of girls quietly talking about that cute boy or what they can wear tomorrow so they can match each other. The majority of the boys are in more of a pack than a pocket. They're rowdy and loud and trying to act 10 years older than they are. Then, there are the stragglers, the loners. You know the ones: too shy to walk with that cute girl and not cool enough to walk with the pack. Well, that's how it was that day as I watched from my throne...the leader of the pack had a loud mouth and a football. He took aim at one of the loners, hitting him on the back of the head. The quarterback broke into a riotous laughter and, of course, was joined by the rest of the pack. They maybe didn't agree with what he did, but would never voice their displeasure with their leader, lest they be walking home with the loner tomorrow. The loner never said a word...probably used to the harsh treatment...hopefully heading to a home that is filled with love, acceptance, and encouragement.

In one fleeting, regal moment, I wanted to run down from my throne and smack that quarterback silly, putting him in his place. I wanted to be a champion for the loner. I wanted to encourage the rest of the pack to abandon their leader and to side with the loner...to show some integrity. Of course, I knew that wouldn't be my place and also that it wouldn't do any good. No, my intervention was not the answer. The key to shaping the character of all these boys rests in the hands of their families. The loner needs to be able to go home and feel safe and secure. He needs to know that he is special...that he has value and worth. The quarterback may be hard on other kids because he's never been taught the value of people. Maybe he has a low self-esteem and doesn't know any other way to be. The rest of the pack needs to learn to stick up for others, realizing that maybe someday they'll need someone to stick up for them. Most of all, these boys need to learn that they are not alone.

The Bible is full of examples of godly men who started out as...boys! Paul was a spiritual bully until the Spirit of God got hold of him, transforming him into a mighty forefather of the Christian faith. Peter was a headstrong, loudmouthed fisherman until he aligned his will with God's and was able to perform miracles. David was a timid little shepherd boy, but his faith in his God gave him the courage to kill a giant and go on to be the greatest king of Israel. Jonathan defied his father because he knew the importance of being faithful not only to God, but to his friend, David.

Boys need to learn that if they put their faith in God, He will be with them every step of the way...and isn't that something we all need to learn? Leaders, followers, loners, boys, girls, men, and women...God is there for all that put their faith in Him.

The Quick Trip

I t was just supposed to be a quick trip: first to the bank and then to the Post Office. Had it been a nice day, we could've walked, but this was an exceptionally cold day. I was home alone with Caleb and the girls had to stay after school for play practice. So, we bundled up to brave the cold because these errands needed to be run today. The "bundling up" process is exactly as it indicates: a process. I took Caleb's slippers off (which he wears around the house all winter) and put on his shoes, tying them in a double knot. Next, I put on his coat and zippered it up. Then came the hat, hood, scarf, and mittens (neatly tucked up under his sleeves), in that order. Now that Caleb was ready, it was time for my coat, which zippers and snaps, my gloves, car keys and purse. I grabbed the items for my banking as well as the 10 Valentine packages and four postcards to be mailed. I managed to shut the door and we made our way to the garage. (Are you tired yet? Just wait, it gets better!)

I had to open the van door so that I could put down all the things I was carrying. Then, I had to lift Caleb up and get him into his car seat, taking off my gloves so I could manage all of the necessary straps and buckles. Replacing my gloves, I shut the door to the van and made my way to the driver's seat. It only takes one minute (or less) to drive to the bank and by the time I pulled in and parked, Caleb had his mittens off. I took my gloves off in order to un-strap him from the car seat, put his mittens back on (tucking them neatly under his sleeves) and put mine back on as well. We gathered our banking items and got out of the van. As we got into the bank, I told Caleb to leave his mittens on because we weren't going to be long. Of course, there was a line...

Kids learn early on how to "work the crowd." They know that the tellers give lollipops and the customer service people on the platform give pretzel rods. While we were waiting for our turn, Caleb asked if he could go ask for a pretzel. I said yes, reminding him to say please and thank you. Unfortunately, in order to do this, he had to go behind me, so I had to periodically look back to check on him while moving along with the line. I guess it's hard to eat a pretzel with mittens on, so off they came. Also, he didn't want to get crumbs on his scarf, so that was the

God doesn't want us to be burdened. He wants us to be free to enjoy the life that He has given us.

next to go. The hat makes him itchy and we were in there long enough for his coat to make him warm. By the time my banking was done (which really wasn't that long), I had to put Caleb's coat back on, zippering it up. Then, I had to put on his hat, hood, scarf, and mittens (tucked neatly under his sleeves), in that order. We got back out to the van where I opened the door, lifted him in, climbed in myself, shut the door, put him in his seat, removed my gloves, fastened him in, replaced my gloves and got into my seat! (Don't get too excited, we're not going home yet. At least you're just reading about these escapades instead of doing them!) I must've sighed, because Caleb asked me what was wrong and I told him that nothing was wrong, I was just tired.

Off to the Post Office we went. I parked the van, took off my gloves in order to deal with that car seat, only to find that Caleb had taken off his hat and mittens again! I took a deep breath and smiled, getting him out of his seat and all bundled up again. I put on my gloves and grabbed the 10 packages and four post cards, my purse and Caleb. We hop out of the van and I desperately try to lock the van, hold on to my things and keep an eye on Caleb in the busy parking lot. We get into the Post Office and, you guessed it, there's a line. By the time I'm done, I have to re-bundle Caleb, once again as well as put him in that ridiculous car seat! Who invented those things anyway? (This coming from Miss "always wear your seat belt-they save lives!") I get him fastened in and put my gloves back on and sit down telling him that we'll be home in a minute and warning him not to remove any article of clothing or else...

In the midst of the many other things I was thinking, I was dreaming about the day when nice weather would be here, when Caleb could go outside in shorts and sandals and we could walk to do our errands. No coats, hats, scarves, mittens, or car seats necessary! Even though the car seat and the many items of warm clothing are annoying at times, they are necessary for Caleb's safety and protection. But there's always that dream when they won't be necessary...

Recently, Chuck has been preaching a series of sermons about all the unnecessary baggage we carry around...things such as self-reliance, loneliness, wounds, fear, harsh words and criticism, anxiety and worry, guilt, doubts, etc. The burden of outerwear will pass in a few months. The burden of a car seat will pass in a few years. The burdens that we carry around inside ourselves will only pass when we choose to give them up to God. Psalm 68:19 says, *"Praise be to the Lord, to God our Savior, who daily bears our burdens."* Psalm 55:22 says, *"Cast your cares on the Lord and He will sustain you; He will never let the righteous fall."*

God doesn't want us to be burdened. He wants us to be free to enjoy the life that He has given us. That freedom only comes when we surrender all of our burdens over to Him.

By the way, we finally made it home that day and the next day...we stayed home in our slippers and played games...no burdens!

Broken Crayons

The other day, I was watching the son of some friends and while his older brother played a game with Charlie and Caitlin, I encouraged him to do some coloring. I gave him a stack of coloring books and an old lunch box full of crayons. When he opened the lunch box, he noticed that a lot of the crayons were broken. He wasn't sure that he could color with the broken pieces and he thought that we should throw some of them away. I got down on his level and showed him that even though these weren't as nice as new crayons can be, they still had very pretty colors and could still be used to make very pretty pictures.

In thinking about those crayons, I imagine that there are times when we all feel a little like those broken pieces. We wonder if people look at us and consider the possibility that we're past the point of being useful. Well, I can tell you that God looks at the broken pieces of our lives and He sees all of the rich color that we have and He envisions all of the beautiful pictures that we have yet to make. Just like the crayons in the box, we each have our own unique color.

In the Bible, we read in Romans 12 that God has given us all different gifts and that we are to use those gifts in harmony with one another. Think about it…a picture is much more interesting when many colors are used to make it. God needs all of us in order to make the picture that He has in mind. We simply need to place our lives in His hand and let Him "do the coloring."

So, next time you see a bunch of broken crayons, think of all the wonderful ways in which they've already been used and then think about all of the wonderful pictures that are yet to come. Let's let God use us to create a beautiful picture together!

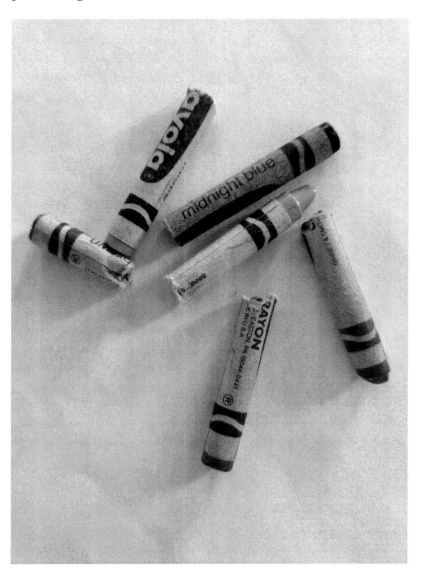

Our Witness

I'd like to talk about something that's of importance to all of us: our witness. Now, some may not even know what this means.

Webster says that a witness is one who testifies. As Christians, we are testifying to the fact that Jesus Christ is the Son of God. That through Him, and only through Him, we can have a personal relationship with God the Father and spend eternity with Him in Heaven when our earthly life is over.

We need to testify to the fact that Jesus died on the cross to pay for our sins and that He rose from the dead only as God could do. We need to testify to the fact that anyone, no matter what they've

Let others know what God has done for you and what He can do for them.

done in the past, can receive this unique salvation if they will only admit their sins and believe that all this is true. And we need to testify to the fact once we've done this, the Holy Spirit will come into our lives and help us to be the best person we can be.

But you can only testify to something that you, yourself, have experienced. So, if you haven't experienced God's love in this way, that's the first step you need to take. If you have, then you need to be a witness for Him. Let others know what God has done for you and what He can do for them.

Sometimes we are called to actually verbalize our faith, but each and every day we are His witnesses by the way we live our lives. When people know we are Christians, they watch us to see how we act, what we do, what we say – even the expression on our face is part of our witness.

Now, I'm not saying that if you're a Christian, there should always be a smile on your face. John 11:35 says that "Jesus wept." But if we go around with scowls or frowns all the time and are always quick to point out the negative aspects of a situation – that can hurt our witness!

In closing, if you don't know Jesus as your personal Savior, ask Him into your life now. If you do know Him, let His life and love shine from you so that you can be a light which leads others to Him.

Ever Have a Day Like That?

The kitchen floor is <u>NOT</u> fit to eat from, the hamper is overflowing, the kids have been writing their names in the dust on the furniture and the sink is full of dirty dishes because the dishwasher is full of clean ones that need to be put away! Ever have a day like that?

I get the kids off to school and think, "Well, I've got my work cut out for me, but I can do it!" But as I walk past the coffee table and see my Bible, I hear the Lord calling to me to spend some time with Him. So, with my Bible read and my prayers said, I begin to tackle the housework – when the phone rings – someone just needs to talk. When I finally hang up, I survey the task at hand and decide which job is most important, since I no longer have time to do it all. Since we have to have clothes to wear, I decide to start with the laundry and as I begin to sort, the doorbell rings – someone wants to visit! Ever have one of those days?

As my friend leaves and I begin to close the door, I hear the bus coming down the road – school is over and now there's homework to help with, books to be read and games to play – not to mention figuring out what suppers' going to be. Ever have a day like that? I hope so, because what makes a house a home is <u>not</u> the cleaning, but the caring.

Priorities- we all need to decide what's really important and the easy way to do that is to ask ourselves this question: "What would Jesus do?"

The <u>house</u>work can wait, the <u>home</u>work can't.

Thank God for Differences

I didn't grow up in Church...in fact, from 4th grade to 10th grade, I didn't go at all, but in 10th grade, we started going to this wonderful Church...and it was there that I began my walk of faith with God. Over the 2 ½ years that I had at that Church before I went to college, I was blessed with godly adults who nurtured that faith in Sunday School, Youth Fellowship, Young Life and worship times. My faith flourished, my knowledge of the Bible grew and my desire to share God's love with others became characteristic of my new life in Christ! Church was my favorite place to be and I can't recall even one negative experience during that time.

I've been a Christian now for 38 years and have been in a total of 10 Churches...and I wish I could say that I'd still never had any negative experiences, but that would be untrue...and unrealistic as well. Max Lucado said: "What makes a Christian a Christian is not perfection but forgiveness!" Churches are made up of people...all different kinds of people with all different ways of thinking. These people aren't perfect...just forgiven...or maybe in need of forgiveness. Maybe, instead of letting these differences cause a conflict, we need to thank God for the differences...for the variety. We need to thank God that He doesn't demand or even expect that we be perfect and we need to thank Him that we can't be...because in seeing our imperfections...we also see our need for Him!

I Like Math

I like math and one of my favorite Christmas gifts was a magazine called *Math Puzzles and Logic Problems* by DELL. I would love to be able to find a cozy corner and curl up with this magazine for a few hours, my only other needs being a large supply of iced tea and a reliable pencil sharpener.

Unfortunately, the demands of church, family and home don't allow me this indulgence. I have to be satisfied with stolen minutes here and there, which is okay because in the scheme of things, logic problems are not that important. However, when solving logic problems, it's much easier when you can do it on a continuous basis...getting into the rhythm. Once you establish a pattern, you also establish the flow.

Life is a lot like solving logic problems and, therefore, so is our Christian walk. Our walk with the Lord is much easier when we do it on a continuous basis! Once we establish a pattern, we will also establish the flow.

Now, I won't waste time explaining how to solve a logic problem because remember: "In the scheme of things, logic problems are not that important." However, I will give some suggestions on how to establish a pattern in our Christian walk.

Assuming the presence of faith, one of the most important ingredients is consistency. As Christians, we should want to read the Bible and pray. This should be done consistently on a daily basis. We also should want to worship the Lord and fellowship with other believers.

Hebrews 10:25 says, *"Let us not give up meeting together, as some are in the habit of doing, but let us encourage one another...and all the more as you see The Day approaching."* Think of the many excuses we hear as to why people miss church. I wonder how many people realize that when The Day approaches, we'll have to explain all those excuses to our Lord face to face. Stolen minutes of our time may be okay when solving logic problems but not when we're talking about time spent with our Lord.

Make a promise to spend time with God. Establish a pattern and watch out for the flow!

Caitlin's Birthday Letter

My Mommy! It is hard to come up with the words to describe my thankfulness for you. I know my life wouldn't be what it is today if it weren't for your constant giving, selflessness, love, and forgiveness. And of course, your example of Christ. You and Dad both always did (and still do) your best to see we are walking with God and being like Jesus, to family and strangers.

Even though we didn't have much money growing up, we were richly blessed. It is because of your willingness to give to others and your giving hearts and tithing no matter what our financial circumstance that God enabled us to still have and do so much! This is probably the best example you showed us (at least to me). Just by living by the Word and having open hearts you led us by example that we can always trust in God to provide for us. It is for that reason I truly never worry about money! So, thank you!

Some memories that I have and cherished moments are things I hope bless you! They are not all "Memories" but just things you did as my Mom that were special to me! I have always loved being "your Caitlin" and always felt extra special because of our little saying! I have even started calling Grace "My Grace" to carry on something so close to my heart. I just thought it was the most thoughtful and exciting thing when I would come home from school and there would be a new shirt or something waiting for me on my bed. It let me know that you were thinking of me even when you weren't with me and of course – getting new clothes is always fun!

Same goes for washing my blankie unexpectedly. It was always so great to snuggle up with a good smelling blankie at bedtime! There was nothing like coming home to fresh baked cookies or bread too! I think of this anytime I'm making something yummy, in hopes to bringing a smile to Scott's face when he gets home from work. You always made time to play double solitaire with me or Scattergories when no one else wanted to. This, of course, meant the world to me and are irreplaceable memories and feelings of love because that is my love language!

Same goes for our annual walk on the beach to walk until we seemed fit and to look for the prettiest purple shells on the shore. I will always cherish that special time with you! I know I can be hard to shop with because of my indecisiveness but every now and then if I am out in the evening shopping, I always think of you. Whether it was getting something I needed last minute or just going to some stores for fun...Fashion Bug and Kohls, Hills and even Giant Eagle. I loved going to those places with you!

I really loved the year we went to Women of Faith and we ate at Cheesecake and shopped at Station Square! I wish we got to shop together more often and hope that can change in the future! I have loved our special dates to the Benedum in recent years and of course the three Women of Faith conferences we got to go to together. What a special time, setting apart those days to spend together and be in God's restoring presence! Thank you for always making birthdays, little holidays, and Christmas so fun and special. I know you passed that down from Grandma and I plan on keeping that "tradition" alive! I can't imagine a life where those special days aren't extra special. Even though it makes you sad to think about our Easter dresses, I'm going to bring them up anyways. I <u>always</u> loved our special dresses and couldn't wait for Easter Sunday to wear them all decked out with either gloves or purple shoes! They were always so different from each other and yet all so beautiful. I know we both felt like princesses wearing them! And even though we don't still have the dresses, we have the memories of wearing them and twirling in them! Thank you for all of the time and energy you put into making them!

Something I always loved was going to craft shows with you! I, of course, still love going now but I especially mean selling stuff with you! It was such a fun special Mom and Daughter time with either just you and me or all three of us girls. I always loved the little snacks you would make us filled with chocolate chips and cheerios and all kinds of other yummy things.

I am so thankful for you always keeping our house so clean and for always having home-cooked meals for us. Neither of those things is an easy task but you always made it happen. Thank you for constantly helping me with all of my cooking questions the past 10 years! Although I don't seem to have a lot of "specific" memories, all of these things make up my childhood and I'm so thankful for all of them!

I loved our beach vacations so much growing up and our yearly stop at Bob Evans on the way home or stopping at

McDonald's on the way there, our Dunkin' Donut breakfast one morning and our ice cream night at the Royal Treat Shoppe. You and Dad sure knew how to make things fun and memorable. I loved how predictable our vacations were and greatly missed it when they started to change.

There, of course, are so many great things about our childhood and the fun things we did...these are just my favorites!

Thank you again for always being an amazing example to us in how you treat Dad and others. An example of unconditional love and sacrifice. An everyday example of Christ and for being the only person who could be "My Mommy."

I love you very much and am happy to celebrate all day with you on your 58th birthday! Happy Birthday Mom!

Love, Your Caitlin

School's Out

School's out! The kids are home and we're embarking on another summer of togetherness! That's a good thing...mostly...there are moments...but that's another story!

When the kids were younger, I could count on one thing happening every day: they would be out playing in the back yard and would run in periodically either "dying of thirst" or "starving to death." I would quickly assuage their hunger and thirst and they'd be off again. Now, they're old enough to take care of their own drinks and snacks, but when they were little, they depended on me to fill their needs.

In Matthew, Chapter 5, we find the Beatitudes, one of which says, *"Blessed are those who hunger and thirst after righteousness, for they will be filled."* Jesus promises that if we truly have a desire to be righteous, He'll fill our needs. Just as the kids knew without a doubt that I would feed their physical hunger and thirst, we can know without a doubt that Jesus will feed our spiritual hunger and thirst. Also, just as the kids had to come in and ask, so we must approach the throne of grace and make our desires known to God through prayer.

It's a good thing that the kids are old enough to get their own drinks and snacks, but may they never feel that they're old enough to fill their own spiritual needs. No matter how old we get, we always need Jesus.

Have a "thirsty" summer!

Pulling The Dog

When it comes to giving toys to our kids (when they were little) and now to our grandkids, I prefer to give gifts that are good for them. You know, ones that are educational or that require some imagination, ones that encourage exercise or that aid in their spiritual growth. I'd rather give gifts like books and board games instead of things that take batteries! I like our gifts to be something they'll treasure...like a keepsake...or nostalgic, which is why we gave our grandkids little toy dogs on a leash...and they love them. I enjoy watching them walk around in circles, pulling that dog behind them, knowing that they're in charge of where that dog goes...there's nothing cuter.

Now, imagine your child pulling you around on a leash...being in charge of where you go and how you spend your time. That wouldn't be so cute! (Although, that's unfortunately how it is with some families, but that's for another article!)

Let's take that thought one step further. Imagine us pulling God around on a leash, being in charge of where He goes and how He spends His time. When we think about it that way, it sounds outrageous...but we may be guilty of that very thing without even realizing it. After all, the last thing that Jesus says in the Gospel of Matthew is that He will be with us always. We claim that promise and trust that He will be our constant companion in the good times and bad...and rightly so. However, when we expect Him to follow us around wherever we go, being subject to our every whim, tagging along while we make too many poor choices...we have a skewed concept of who God really is and the kind of relationship He desires to have with us.

In John 12:26, Jesus says, *"Whoever serves Me must follow Me; and where I am, My servant also will be. My Father will honor the one who serves Me."* If we keep our eyes focused on Him and follow His leading, He will not only be with us...and we with Him, but we will be honored by the Father. God is to be served and followed...that's who He is. He wants to guide us on the path in life that's best for us...one where He is honoring us by His presence. That's the kind of relationship He desires to have with us.

Emily and Daniel can have fun with their dogs, but they can't have a relationship with them. It's all one-sided! Follow the One True God who could've chosen to leave it one-sided, but instead chose to give us His love and guidance so that we can enjoy a relationship with Him that will take us, not around in circles, but into eternity with Him!

Couldn't Wait to Tell You

I remember when we found out that we were expecting for the first time. I wasn't even two months along, but we couldn't wait to share our news...with anyone who had an ear to hear!

We began to prepare...there were classes to take and showers to be had. We had to paint the room and pick the names...it was an exciting time!

We also needed to make sure that we were nurturing this new life. I needed to watch what I ate and I needed to take special vitamins. I tried to steer clear of places and practices that would be harmful to this new life inside of me. We were told that we needed to take care throughout the pregnancy, but that the most vulnerable time was during the first trimester...the early stage.

When Charlie was born and as he grew, we knew how important it was to build on the good foundation that we had given him. We taught him the benefits of eating his vegetables and of getting exercise. We also taught him all about God and His love...encouraging him to develop these lessons for himself throughout his entire life.

That was a long time ago...26 years ago this Thanksgiving, as a matter of fact...but I remember it like it was yesterday. I can also remember another special time from my past...when I accepted Christ as my Savior. It was such an exciting time and I couldn't wait to share the Good News...with anyone who had an ear to hear!

I had a wonderful support system at my church so that my new life in Christ was nurtured and cared for during that vulnerable early stage. I was taught that I needed to develop good habits of worshipping, praying, studying the Word, and sharing my faith and that I needed to learn to steer clear of places and practices that could harm my new faith. I was encouraged to develop these new habits throughout my entire walk of faith.

In 1 Peter 3:15, we are told to always be prepared to give a reason for the hope that we have...so ask me sometime about Jesus...I'd love to share Him with you. Also, even after 26 years, I'm still not tired of talking about my kids. I've always got pictures to show, stories to tell and good news to share...like that Carrie and Ben are expecting their first child and that when she wasn't even two months along, they couldn't wait to share their news...with anyone who had an ear to hear!

Pruning

Give me a bare wall and I can fill it with pictures and shelves and candles in a very appealing way (if I do say so myself) but put me out in the yard and I'm at a loss as to how to "decorate" it. The flare I have inside the home is lost when I go outside. Needless to say, I'm very impressed with people who have well-manicured and intricately landscaped properties. Although we make an attempt at "keeping up appearances," I am sure that any gardener enthusiast could find many flaws in our program. We do the usual and expected, like cutting the grass and keeping up with the weeds. We even plant a few summer flowers, but that's the extent of it.

This past spring, however, we decided to prune the grapevine. We had never done anything with it and weren't sure how long it had been. We followed a guide about pruning (as much as a "lay-gardener" can) and

Be patient and wait for the growth. The harvest of joy you reap will be worth the pain of the pruning

prune we did! We cut that vine back until it seemed as though there was nothing left. Then, we waited. Little by little, a few leaves appeared and now it seems to be as full as it was before. Some people (you know, those green thumb people) may find this quite normal, but I find it amazing!

John 15 talks about Jesus being the Vine, the Father being the gardener and we being the branches. This passage talks about the necessity of pruning in order to be more fruitful. We may have times in our life when we feel as though we've been stripped bare, never to be of much use again.

Take heart. Maybe these are the times when the Father is pruning us, getting rid of the old hard parts of our lives so that the parts that are growing can do so more efficiently. Be patient and wait for the growth. The harvest of joy you reap will be worth the pain of the pruning.

Giving

Picture this commercial: Soldiers coming out of their tents in a place like Iraq or Afghanistan...and it's snowing! They're amazed and excited! Then picture a little boy who has just gotten off Santa's lap and an elf asks him what he asked for...and the little boy smiles and says, "Something for my Dad." Now, I don't know about you, but that's the kind of thing that always makes me cry...and I don't even know what they were advertising!

I'm not sure what your thoughts are on Santa and how he fits into Christmas, but that's not important. What's important is that a little child did a very selfless, compassionate thing...and that's what Christmas is all about...giving of ourselves and doing things for others! When our children were growing up, we encouraged them to only ask Santa for one thing, feeling that the traditional "mile-long" list seemed a tad too greedy. From a child's perspective then, they really needed to make their wish count, because it was the only one they had. The little boy in the commercial obviously felt the same way and so he made sure his wish was a really important one...but not one for himself. He chose to use his wish for someone else...his Dad...who was far away from home, serving his country.

When we put the needs and wants of others before our own, we're showing God's love to the world, following the example set by a little Child so long ago...who grew up and did the ultimate selfless and compassionate thing...gave His life for all of mankind so that we may have the opportunity to be in relationship with God forever.

So, this Christmas, give some of your time to help those less fortunate. Give some of your money to a worthy cause. But most importantly, give yourself to the One who has given you the best gift that you'll ever receive!

Rescued

Much of life is routine: We wake up and get ready for our day of work or school, we eat our meals at the usual time and we go to bed. There are some variations: Maybe we read or watch TV or play a game...which can become routine as well, but every now and then, life surprises us!

Sometimes surprises can be good: "Will you marry me?" "We're going to have a baby." "I got a big promotion today." And sometimes not so good: "I'm afraid it's cancer." "There's been an accident." "Sorry, but our company needs to downsize."

Recently, I asked our Vacation Bible Schoolers to tell me something about God and I was genuinely and pleasantly surprised by some of their answers. First, there was quite an extensive list of the things that God made, that He loves

"I tell you the truth, unless you change and become like little children, you will never enter the kingdom of heaven."

us and died for our sins, which were great answers. Then, if it got a little deeper: God listens to our prayers and He hears our praise. He protects us and loves us even "when we're bad" (I suggested that we change that to "when we do bad things"). Lastly, and most surprisingly, a 4-year-old boy raised his hand and said, "God rescues us" and I almost cried!... *"and a little child shall lead them"* (Isaiah 11:6).

Not surprisingly, we can learn a lot from children. In fact, Jesus said in Matthew 18:3, "*I tell you the truth, unless you change and become like little children, you will never enter the kingdom of heaven.*"

Don't overthink what the Bible has to tell us about God and His love for us. Accept it with the simple faith of a child...and be rescued!

Craft Show and Ice

It seems that more often than not, my monthly epistles have to do with happenings while on the road. Maybe I need to stay at home a little more...

On the first Saturday in December, I had a craft show about 45 minutes south of home. It didn't start until 10:00am, which meant that I could sleep in...under normal circumstances. The night before, we had our first big snow of the season and our big plans for snow tires had yet to materialize. After cleaning off the car, which we had left out the night before because the alley leading to our garage was a sheet of ice, I headed slowly out of town. I made it up the big hill and finally onto the main

God gives us those glimmers of hope...

road, which had been plowed, but was still snow-covered. The snow on the road was very choppy, making for a rough ride. At times, the snow became smooth which I thought would be an improvement, but was slick and, therefore, precarious. Every now and then, I came to a patch of road that was bare: wet, but bare. It was a sunny morning, so those wet, bare patches shone like gold. In the midst of the rough and slippery stretches, I could look up ahead and see those occasional patches of hope. They were a welcome encouragement on a treacherous journey.

Isn't life like that? Sometimes the road is rough and seems to shake our very foundation. Other times, we feel like we could lose control at any minute, sending us off in a dangerous direction. Periodically, God gives us those glimmers of hope where we feel safe and secure, reminding us that He is with us.

In Matthew 28:20, Jesus tells us that He is with us always, and <u>that</u> is a welcome encouragement on a treacherous journey.

This New Year, may you realize Christ's presence with you.

I Love to Read

I love to read and my favorite genre being Christian Historical fiction that takes place between the Civil War and the turn of the century.

I recently finished a book about a young woman named Tarsie who left New York City to live in Kansas. She traveled with her friend Mary, Mary's husband Joss and their two young children. Mary died as soon as they arrived in Kansas, but not before making Tarsie promise to look after her husband and children.

Tarsie strikes up a friendship with a black woman named Ruth and in talking one day, Ruth discovers that Tarsie can read and write and is planning to teach the children. Ruth exclaims how that is such a fine thing to know. Then she notices Tarsie's Bible and says, "You can open that book anytime you please, can't you, and read the words for yourself. That is what I hunger for, to read God's Word for myself...and I want it for my children even more than wanting it for me."

Now I am reading a book where a woman named Clair is teaching a young woman, Sara, to read. As Sara begins to get the hang of it, Clair leaves the room and returns with a large Bible, saying, "This is why we learn to read. It is so we can read Scripture and learn about God's plan for our lives."

I commented to Chuck how both books put such value on reading the Bible and he said, "There's your newsletter article!"

I love reading my Bible and I cannot imagine not being able to read it or anything else! May we never take for granted the gift of reading as well as the gift of God's Word...for it is *"A lamp unto our feet and a light unto our path."* Psalm 119:105

Dirty Face Kiss

Everyday when it is naptime, Caitlin always wants to give Carrie a kiss before going to bed. Today, however, she tried doing so before I had a chance to wipe her up, and Carrie decided that she was not interested in kissing this face with remnants of lunch on it!

In my desire to keep this process going, I told Carrie to kiss her anyway, but she refused. My first instinct was to tell her that the next time <u>her</u> face was dirty I would not kiss her – hoping to speak a little sympathy or compassion. Then, I realized that I should be trying to "spark" the unconditional love that God shows us and that He wants us to show each other.

So, in order to illustrate this quality, I gave Caitlin a kiss (dirty face and all) and then Carrie decided that she could too! The next time you feel that your "face is too dirty" to come to God, remember that He loves you with an unconditional love. He accepts us just as we are. Go to Him as would a child – dirty face and all!

Picnic Grove Tree

Just down the road from where we live is a little picnic grove from days gone by. The ground is level as you venture from the road and then there is a drastic drop down to where a long-neglected table stands. It appears that no one cares for the area, because the grass is high and the brush is overwhelming.

There are trees surrounding the grove...one in particular that is located on the cusp of the precipice. Before the arrival of spring, I noticed that the tree had fallen, not down into the grove, but toward the road. I felt bad for the little tree, assuming that it was dead.

God promises to stand by us and to help us in our time of need.

Recently on one of my morning walks past the grove, I once again saw the little tree, and to my surprise, there were leaves beginning to grow on it. I then noticed that it had not completely fallen but was resting on a near-by tree at about a 45-degree angle...enough to keep its roots intact. I remember thinking how fortunate it was for the little tree that it had a neighbor nearby to help!

God makes many promises to us in His Word. Let me list a few from the book of Psalms. He delivers us (50:15) and saves us (34:18). He sustains us (54:4) and upholds us (63:8). He guards us (91:11) and is our dwelling place

(90:1). He watches over our coming and going both now and forevermore (121:8).

God promises to stand by us and to help us in our time of need. He guards us and upholds us so that our roots remain intact...so that we remain rooted in Him! Sometimes He takes care of us on His own, but sometimes, He uses a nearby neighbor to help!

We need to make sure that we are firmly rooted in God and His love and we need to surround ourselves with godly "neighbors" who will be there to catch us if we fall...and be ready for God to use us to do the same for them!

It's How You Say It

One of the responsibilities of raising children is to teach them right from wrong. Lately, we've been dealing with Charlie in this area. It's not that he's been saying bad things, but rather it's the way in which he says them. I'm sure we can all think of times when we've said things that, in themselves, aren't so bad, but our method of delivery has left a lot to be desired.

Just as we try to teach our children and grandchildren how to be kind in the things that they say and how they say them, so God teaches us through His Word. Proverbs 10:19 refers to the wise person being one who holds his tongue and James 1:26 talks about keeping a tight rein on our tongues.

We need to be always thinking about other people and how our words will affect them. Once we can do this, we'll have learned a valuable lesson that we can truly pass on to others.

Communication

This month, I'd like to talk about communication. Of course, we all know how important communication is to any relationship, and we all realize that without it, we eventually have no relationship at all! What is it that causes us to have a lack of communication with our friends and loved ones? Usually, it's one of two reasons: someone has offended us or we have offended someone. When an offense occurs, thus causing hurt and/or anger, the communication stops. Nothing is resolved and the relationship is strained. If it goes on too long, the relationship may be permanently damaged.

Now, what does God have to say about this problem? In Matthew 5:23-24, He tells us that before we can work on our relationship with Him, we must first right our wrong relationships with others. If we have offended someone, we must first go to that person and confess to them our wrong and ask for their forgiveness. How they choose to respond is up to them. Once we have done our part, we are then free to pursue our relationship to God.

On the other hand, maybe you have been offended by someone. In Matthew 18:15, Jesus tells us to go to our brother and to let him know his offense and forgive him. Once again, how he chooses to respond is up to him but at least we have done our part; the part that God calls us to do.

Either way, we have a responsibility and we must accept that responsibility before we can resume a right-relationship with God.

So, if you're feeling as though God is far away, maybe there's an unconfessed sin or an unforgiving heart blocking the way to a wonderful relationship with Jesus. Take care of things before you come to the altar. Seek God with a pure heart and enjoy unlimited communication with Someone who loves you very much!

Seasons of Life

Fall...cool, crisp mornings, sweet apple cider and, of course...leaves! I love fall! Now, don't get me wrong, I appreciate all of the seasons and, in fact, am really glad that we live in Pennsylvania because we seem to get our fair share of each one! But there's just something special about fall...watching as the leaves change from rich greens to deep reds, vibrant oranges, and sunny yellows...waiting for them to reach their "peak."

In summer, the chlorophyll in the leaves is busy converting carbon dioxide and water to carbohydrates...the food needed by the tree for its growth. Chlorophyll is also what gives the leaves their green color. As we come into fall, that chlorophyll begins to break down because of the longer nights and cooler weather, thus revealing the other pigments that were present in the leaves all along. So, when we stand in awe of autumn's palette...God's artistic creation...we are actually applauding the fact that the leaves have served their purpose...and are on their way out!

People often liken the human life to the seasons...and I guess that in the "seasons of life," I would also be coming into my "fall" years. Although we have many purposes here on earth, I am done serving one purpose: I have given birth to and nursed four children...and those days are definitely behind me. I guess that also means that I, too, am "on my way out"! Hopefully, I still have quite a few years left, but as I marvel at the beauty of the fall that surrounds me, it is my desire to mimic that beauty and to live a life that's ablaze with a color of my own...a color of God's design!

As I think about the colors of fall, some "colorful" women come to mind. I think of Jane with her cheery cards and of Elizabeth with her welcoming smile. I think of Myrtle with her passion for missions and of Mrs. Rightmeyer with her boundless love for children.

I want my life to be rich with color so that I can be a blessing to those around me and a testament to the Artist...the Creator...God!

May this be a blessing to you...and may you, in turn, be a blessing to others.

Healing and Thankfulness

The devotional which I am currently using is called "The One Year Book of Healing" by Dr. Reggie Anderson. It caught my eye when I was shopping at our local Christian bookstore before they went out of business and I immediately thought of my desire to be healed from cancer and so I bought it. I've been reading it for four months now and I've come to realize that healing comes in many forms, dealing with all kinds of issues: physical, spiritual, and emotional.

At the beginning of each month, Dr. Anderson encourages us to do an exercise that helps us heal. In October, it was to do an act of kindness each day and this month, he suggests that we daily think of five things that we're thankful for. I quickly did the math and felt a little overwhelmed at coming up with 150 things to be thankful for...but I've been amazed at just how many things there are. I've been sharing these thankful thoughts on Facebook and I've written about being thankful for everything from people in my life to places I've visited to simple pleasures and even my five senses. I also write about God and His love, grace, mercy, provision, and faithfulness.

The Psalmist tells us to enter His gates with **thanksgiving** and His courts with praise, and Paul tells us to present our requests to God with **thanksgiving** and that we are to **give thanks** in all circumstances!

God's healing comes in His timing and my daily part in that healing process is to offer Him my thanks and praise!

Crocheting

Years ago, my sister taught me to crochet. I made some scarves and several afghans before moving on to other crafts. Over the years, I've tried my hand at making many different things...but, now I'm back to crocheting...once again making scarves, but also prayer shawls and cotton dishcloths. I figure that I could handle more difficult projects, but I enjoy keeping things simple and making things with a purpose! I also enjoy using variegated yarn. I love seeing all the different colors come together to form a beautiful pattern...one strand, strong and united!

That's how I imagine God looking at His church...different people with a variety of gifts and talents to offer. When we fulfill our purpose of spreading a "simple" Gospel, we come together to form a beautiful reflection of God's love...one body, strong and united!

As we celebrate Thanksgiving this month, take some time to think about all the many ways that God has blessed you and be thankful, but also think and pray about all the many ways that you can "give back" to God. What are your gifts and talents and how can you use them to share the Gospel with others...to further His Kingdom here on earth?

Let's work together to make our church a beautiful reflection of God's love...one body, strong and united!

Free Furniture

It was just about time for Caitlin to get out of the crib and we were faced with having to buy yet more bedroom furniture! Just before we did, some friends offered us their grown daughter's furniture: bed, dresser with mirror, chest, nightstand, bookcase, and desk! What an answer to prayer! It was in great shape considering it'd been used for, probably, 15 years. It was just what we needed! Over the years, we had to replace some knobs and the bed went by the wayside, so Carrie had been using our old double bed. Recently, Charlie moved to Florida and Carrie moved into his room and is using his furniture. The double bed is in the "new" guest room and I was eager to get rid of the furniture that had served us for, probably, yet another 15 years.

Unsure as to what to do, we said a prayer over it, hoping that someone who needs it would find it. We put it out in the front yard with a "Free" sign on it. It was

I remember a time when I was in need.... in need of a Savior!

there for, maybe, ½ hour when someone stopped and asked, "Are you sure this is free? My daughter has no furniture and could really use this. Are you sure you won't take anything for it?" I explained that it was given to us and that we were happy to pass it along. "This is just what we need. God Bless You!" she said, and I realized just how much He already has!

I remember a time when I was in need...in need of a Savior! Someone shared their faith with me, telling me of God's love and His free gift of salvation made possible through Jesus, His Son. I prayed a prayer and my life was changed forever...it was just what I needed! Over the years, I've tried to pass God's love along to others: friends, loved ones and even strangers. If you don't know Jesus as your Savior, let me pass Him onto you...He's just what you need!

Playground Promises

I promised Caleb that we would go to the playground. When he pressed me for a time, I decided that after dinner would be the best time to go. It was a Wednesday and Chuck had a service, Caitlin had band practice and, of course, Charlie and Carrie were away at college.

I had put in a busy day at home, so when dinner had come and gone, the last thing I wanted to do was to go to the playground. I presented some alternative options: "How about if we play Candy Land?" or "Why don't we do some puzzles?" Unfortunately (or so I thought), those sedentary suggestions were met with a resistant disappointment and so, off we went. After all, a promise is a promise.

On the walk over, I explained to Caleb that I was tired and that I wasn't going to play *with* him, just watch him play. I was going to sit on a bench, reading my book while sipping my iced tea. This arrangement seemed to be working out just fine...for the first five minutes. There's certain playground equipment that a 4-year-old is capable of handling all by himself and other equipment that looms largely in his eyes. Straight across monkey bars are a cinch, while loop-de-loop ones are a puzzlement. Strap swings are easy, while tire swings are not. And you know those little merry-go-rounds that you run with and jump on...?

No matter how hard or easy, each piece of the equipment came with a "Look, Mommy!" or a "Come and see this!" So, I showed him how to do the things that he couldn't figure out and I marveled at the things that he *could* do by himself. I listened to the delighted squeals as I pushed him on the tire swing. I eavesdropped as the captain of the ship braved a mighty storm (that took place on one of those wooden all-in-one structures).

Psalm 149:4 says that "*the Lord takes delight in His people.*" In Deuteronomy 31:6, the Lord says, "*I will never leave you nor forsake you.*" Jesus says in Matthew 28:20, "*I am with you always.*"

Fortunately, my sedentary suggestions were met with a resistant disappointment and I was able to see how much I am needed and I was able to take delight in my child. Our heavenly Father gives us a perfect example of parenting. May we always seek to follow that example and take delight in our children.

Germs

Clean hands have become the #1 priority in our lives...and not only our hands, we clean our clothes when we have been out and our steering wheels. We clean our phones and our credit cards and even the groceries that we bring home.

We have become hyper-sensitive to the germs that surround us on the outside...but what about the "germs" that reside within? What about the germs of discontent, complaining, arguing, barking politicians, using God's name in inappropriate ways?

Have we been so busy cleaning the outside, that we have neglected to clean the inside as well? Jesus says in Matthew, chapter 15, that "*eating with unwashed hands does not make (someone) unclean, but the things that come out of the mouth come from the heart, and these can make (someone) unclean.*"

David poses this question in Psalm 24: "*Who may ascend the hill of the Lord? Who may stand in His holy place? He who has clean hands and a pure heart, who does not lift up his soul to an idol or swear by what is false.*"

So, how do we go about cleaning our hearts? David shows us how in Psalm 51. He prays: "*Create in me a clean (pure) heart, O God, and renew a right (steadfast) spirit within me.*"

Spend some time in prayer, talk to God and ask Him to make your heart clean and pure and be amazed at the blessings you will receive and pass it on to others!

Abrams-Hildbold vows said

Harbison Chapel, Grove City College, was the setting for the marriage ceremony of Cheryl Anne Abrams and Charles Franklin Hildbold, Jr. The couple exchanged wedding vows during a double-ring ceremony officiated by the Reverends John C. Boor of Johnstown, and Barry J. Brown of Shelton, Conn. Two vases of assorted spring flowers were on the altar and white bows marked the pews. The chancel was decorated with live foliage and two candelabra. Holy Communion was observed with the exchanging of vows. The organist was Mrs. Marian Sautter of Grove City; the soloist was the groom's father, Charles Hildbold Sr.

The bride is the daughter of Mr. and Mrs. William F. Brown of Ithaca, N.Y. The groom's parents are Mr. and Mrs. Charles F. Hildbold of 147 Manchester Drive, Irwin.

When given in marriage by her father, the bride wore a gown of silk organza trimmed with reembroidered lace. The gown featured a scoop neckline, a lace and pearl covered bodice which had long, tapered sleeves ending in points over her hands. Her full skirt was bordered with reembroidered lace and extended to a chapel length train. She wore a Juliet head piece with a finger tip veil including a blusher and carried her mother's white Bible, a long stemmed white rose and a lace handkerchief all combined with white ribbon and streamers.

Maid of honor was the groom's cousin, Janice Garrity of Toledo, Ohio, who wore a long pastel yellow gown which featured a scoop neckline, off the shoulder sleeves and an A-line full skirt. Over the gown she wore a yellow chiffon jacket with lace trimming.

carried a wicker basket with an arrangement including silk daisies and carnations, baby's breath, greens and a green silk bow and streamers. She had daisies and baby's breath in her hair.

The bridemaids were Jane Bankson of Oil City; Nancy Richardson of Derry; Deborah Stocker of Ithaca, N.Y. all friends of the bride, and Ellen Hildbold of Irwin, sister of the groom. They all wore pastel green gowns of the same style as that of the maid of honor and carried baskets of the same types of floral arrangement, only with yellow ribbon and streamers. They also wore daisies and baby's breath in their hair.

Best man was David Fredenburgh of Pittsburgh. The ushers included Grant Abrams, Jr., brother of the bride; Bryon Campbell of Irwin; Roderick Paul of Kane, and Gregory Spalding of Pittsburgh, all friends of the groom.

The mother of the bride chose a beige street length dress. She wore a corsage of yellow silk roses. The mother of the groom wore a street length dress of a rose shade and had a wrist corsage of off-white silk roses.

A reception was held immediately following the ceremony at Grace United Methodist Church of Grove City. Present were family and friends from Pennsylvania, New York, Connecticut, Maryland, Ohio and Arizona. The groom's sister, Sally L. Hildbold, was the guest book attendant.

The bride is a 1976 graduate of Lansing High School, Lansing, N.Y. and a 1980 graduate of Grove City College.

The groom is a 1975 graduate of Hempfield Area Senior High School and a 1979 graduate of Grove City

Mrs. Charles Franklin Hildbold, Jr.

his second year at United Theological Seminary in Dayton, Ohio. He will also serve as the Student Associate Pastor of the Faith United Methodist Church of

Middletown, Ohio.

Following a honeymoon trip to Nags Head, North Carolina, the couple will reside at 1515 First Avenue, Middletown, Ohio.

New Year Advice

Many people think of a new year as a new beginning...a fresh start. Maybe during the past year, we experienced illness and we're hoping that with the new year will come a return to health. Maybe we experienced the loss of a loved one and we're hoping for a further healing of our wounds. Maybe we're encouraged by this fresh start to read the books we've been meaning to read, to exercise and watch our diet, to be more patient and kind.

There are many hopes placed upon this new year...and that's good. God wants us to have hopes and dreams and to set goals for ourselves. He wants the best for us! We need to remember this because sometime during this new year full of promises, our hopes and dreams may be shattered. We may find ourselves asking the question: Why do bad things happen to good people? We might even find ourselves blaming God and that's when we need to remember that he wants the best for us.

Here are some Scriptures to help you through these times:

- *"For the Lord watches over the righteous."* (Psalm 1:6a)

- *"I can do all things through Christ who gives me strength."* (Philippians 4:13)

- *"God will give relief to you who are troubled."* (2 Thessalonians 1:7a)

- *"And even the very hairs of your head are numbered."* (Matthew 10:30)

- *"And my God will meet all your needs according to His glorious riches in Christ Jesus."* (Philippians 4:19)

- *"No temptation has seized you except what is common to men. And God is faithful; He will not let you be tempted beyond what you can bear. But when you are tempted, He will also provide a way out so that you can stand up under it."* (1 Corinthians 10:13)

- *"Humble yourselves, therefore, under God's mighty hand, that He may lift you up in due time, cast all your anxiety on Him because He cares for you."* (1 Peter 5:6-7)

- *"The eternal God is your refuge, and underneath are the everlasting arms. He will drive out your enemy before you saying, 'Destroy him!'"* (Deuteronomy 33:27)

- *"Let us not become weary in doing good, for at the proper time we will reap a harvest if we do not give up."* (Galatians 6:9)

- *"Therefore, I tell you, whatever you ask for in prayer, believe that you have received it, and it will be yours."* (Mark 11:24)

- *"Give, and it will be given to you. A good measure, pressed down, shaken together, and running over, will be poured into your lap. For with the measure you use, it will be measured to you."* (Luke 6:38)

- *"But those who hope in the Lord will renew their strength. They will soar on wings like eagles; they will run and not grow weary; they will walk and not be faint."* (Isaiah 40:31)

- *"When you pass through the waters, I will be with you, and when you pass through the rivers, they will not sweep over you. When you walk through the fire, you will not be burned; the flames will not set you ablaze."* (Isaiah 43:2)

- *"So do not fear, for I am with you; do not be dismayed, for I am your God. I will strengthen you and help you; I will uphold you with my righteous right hand."* (Isaiah 41:10)

- *"Being confident of this, that He who began a good work in you will carry it on to completion until the day of Christ Jesus."* (Philippians 1:6)

- *"When Jesus spoke again to the people He said, 'I am the light of the world. Whoever follows me will never walk in darkness but will have the light of life.'"* (John 8:12)

- *"If any of you lacks wisdom, he should ask God, who gives generously to all without finding fault and it will be given to him."* (James 1:5)

- *"And we know that in all things God works for the good of those who love Him, who have been called according to His purpose. For those God foreknew He also predestined to be conformed to the likeness of His Son, that He might be the firstborn among many brothers."* (Romans 8:28-29)

So, when you hope your hopes and dream your dreams, remember that God loves you very much and will be by your side in the good times and in the bad times. He will carry you!

Choices

"**M**om, can I stay home from school today?" "Don't you feel well, honey?" "Oh, I feel fine. I just don't feel like going." "Okay, Sweetie, whatever you want."

"Dad, I don't feel like going to the dentist today." "But honey, you didn't go with us last time." "I know. I'll go again sometime." "Well, as long as you promise to go sometime."

What were your thoughts as you read these paragraphs? Probably they were something like, "What's wrong with these parents? How can they allow their children to make such important decisions?"

Let's look at the reverse situation. "Mom, I feel really sick. Maybe I should go to see the doctor." "Oh, you're fine. It's just your imagination. Besides, I'm too busy to take you to see the doctor."

"Dad, Dad, wake up! It's almost time for the school bus and I'm not dressed and I haven't had any breakfast." "Oh well, so you'll miss school today. It's more important for us to catch up on our sleep." "But Dad, I've already missed two days this week and I'll be so far behind." "You won't use half the stuff they make you learn anyway. Don't worry about it. Go back to bed."

Again, I would imagine that you're shocked by these words. What terrible parents...denying their children the things they need to be healthy, growing individuals.

A good parent would never allow their children to decide whether or not they go to school or to the dentist. Right? A good parent makes sure that their children get to the doctor as soon as they see the need. Good parents even take their children for a check-up, just to make sure everything is okay. Right? Good parents encourage their children in the schooling process...making sure that they're up in plenty of time, getting a good breakfast, are clothed properly and have their homework done. Right?

Why are we so careful to see to all of our children's needs...except for one? Somehow it doesn't shock us so much to hear these words: "Mom, I don't feel like going to Sunday school." "Okay, dear, whatever you want." "Dad, Dad, wake up! We're going to be late for Sunday school!" "It's okay, son...it's more important for us to catch up on our sleep..."

We have many choices to make in life. Joshua 24:15 says, *"Choose you this day whom you will serve...as for me and my house, we will serve the Lord."*

Be sure you make the right choice!

Marriage and the Handsome Prince

For as young as she is, Carrie often thinks about what her life will be like when she's older. She thinks about getting married – and whom she is going to marry changes frequently. I try to reassure her that when she's old enough, she'll meet a nice man who loves Jesus and they'll get married and live happily ever after.

The picture I paint sounds very much like a fairy tale – but I guess that's what mothers want for their daughters (and sons).

Realistically, I realize that life is not a fairy tale and it's impossible for me to write my daughter's future – but I do have a very influential contribution to that future. As a mother and a Christian, I realize the importance of teaching my children as well as setting a good example for them. But, also, as I'm learning more and more each day, I realize the importance of praying for my children – not just for the day or the near future, but for the distant future – for that time when they possibly will marry and also for the "handsome prince" who may come riding into their lives.

God's People

When I was younger, before I knew Jesus Christ as my Lord and Savior, Easter was just another holiday - a time for gathering with family, wearing new clothes, and hunting for Easter eggs. Now, all of these things are great and we really enjoyed ourselves, but we were missing the real meaning of this special time of the year.

Recently, I was listening to a song called "God's People" by Scott Wesley Brown. It is one that I would like to sing in church, but for now, I'd like to share some of the words with you.

In the song, God's people are described as being patient, kind, loving, servants, builders, and those who reach out to others. They are described as ones

"Are you, am I, are we God's People?"

who grant mercy, seek peace, are gracious, give comfort, bring hope, and encourage others.

The chorus goes on to say: "Are you, am I, are we God's people? Or do we just go through the motions and say the words? Our lives declare Him like banners unfurled. God's people are so needed in this world."

When I became a Christian, Easter took on its proper meaning. I became one of God's people. But, as I listen to the words of this song, I am forced to examine my life as one of God's people. Am I just going through the motions, knowing all the right words to say? And when the banner of my life is unfurled, what does it declare?

Are <u>you</u>, am <u>I</u>, are <u>we</u> God's people? Please take some time to examine your life. Be one of God's people and experience the real meaning of Easter!

Dandelions

The other day, Carrie and Caitlin were out in the backyard cleaning up after our dog, Lou, a job that always needs to be done before Charlie can cut the grass. Carrie and I had noticed how quickly the dandelions had grown up, seemingly overnight! In fact, all of the weeds seemed to be sprouting up in full force.

I looked out to see how the girls were doing and I happened to catch Carrie as she wielded her scoop like a machete, sending the dried-up heads of the dandelions into oblivion, only to have them come to rest (you guessed it!) back on our lawn, in more places than when she started. In her childish, nonprofessional attempt to rid our yard of dandelions, she single-handedly gave us more.

Our lives can be a little like our yard. The weeds of sin can spring up overnight and take over our lives if they're not dealt with in the proper way. Just as a yard will do better with a little fertilizer and weed killer, so will our lives be if we fertilize with worship, devotions, and prayer.

So, as you take time this Spring caring for your lawn, remember to take time to care for your life as well. Remembering that when we try to deal with sin in our own way instead of God's way, we end up in worse shape than when we started.

Random Acts of Kindness

Random acts of kindness. Most of us have heard of them. We've maybe even done them...or had them done to us. Sometimes they're planned, but most times, they just happen...unexpectedly and at random!

Chuck and I recently took a trip to Yorktown and Jamestown in Virginia. We also toured Harper's Ferry, West Virginia and Antietam, Maryland. We wanted to use our National Park's Pass before it expired!

We enjoyed walking through history and even did some hefty climbing... if you've ever been to Harper's Ferry and climbed to Jefferson Rock, you know what I'm talking about! After that climb and descent, we took a moment to have a protein bar and a drink of water on a bench. While there, two families came by with a total of 11 children! We started talking with them and discovered that they were Christians. One family had just moved to North Carolina near Raleigh and we mentioned that our son, Charlie, was interviewing for a job near there and that we were hoping this job would be the answer to many prayers. The North Carolina man offered to pray with us right then and there...and we were so blessed by this unexpected, random act of kindness.

After finishing up at Harper's Ferry, we headed to Antietam, arriving around lunch time. We should have stopped along the way for something to eat because our sparse breakfast and that protein bar were causing us to run on empty...but we didn't. We watched the film about Antietam at the Visitor's Center and got our passport stamped in the bookstore. Then we climbed some stairs to an observation deck, from which you could see the entire battlefield. As we opened the door to the deck, the wonderful aroma of pizza overwhelmed us. We must have appeared to be starving because the nice group of ROTC seniors from IUP offered us each a slice. Once again, we were blessed by the unexpected, random act of kindness!

Look for ways that you can be a blessing to others...even ask God to present you with an opportunity to do just that...but also be open to the time when God will use others to bless you! Random acts of kindness: God's way of revealing Himself through us and to us!

GPS

Have you ever gotten lost? We used to get lost quite a bit, but now with Google Maps on our phones, it doesn't happen as often. Occasionally, however, we're not paying attention and we miss the turn that the GPS wants us to take...and that's when the GPS re-routes us and gets us going in the right direction again! I still like maps for long-distance traveling, but you can't beat a GPS when your journey takes you into a big, unfamiliar city!

We've all heard it said that "Life is a Journey" and when you look at the big picture, our lives consist of many years, which makes it a long-distance journey...therefore, requiring a map, a guide to help you navigate...to show you the right way to go. The Bible is to be our map, our guide...showing us the road that we're to take.

Occasionally, we don't pay attention and we make a wrong turn, a wrong choice and we veer off course, straying from the path that God desires for us to take. Romans 8:28 promises us that *"God works all things together for the good of those who love Him!"* That means that when we make that wrong turn or choice, God is there, just like a GPS, re-routing us and getting us back on track!

You see, God knows each of our journeys. He sees the big picture and wants to make sure that we reach the best destination possible...eternity with Him! So, trust Him and His Word to guide you through this big, unfamiliar life, knowing that He loves us unconditionally and wants the absolute best for us!

Un-Decorating

Every year when I put away the Christmas decorations, I invariably...and possibly purposely forget something. It's usually something small like a refrigerator magnet or a night light. Sometimes it's a towel or potholder that I find in a drawer or this pretty blue plaque with a snowy scene that would be great to leave up all winter except for the fact that it says, "Merry Christmas"! It's frustrating because I just want to get the job done! The problem is, we get so used to having these things around that we fail to notice them...even when they're right in front of us! Usually, I eventually spot these lingering items myself, but sometimes it takes another eye to catch them and bring them to my attention.

Isn't that kind of how it is with our Christian walk? We give our hearts to Jesus who promises to make us into new creations (see 2 Corinthians 5:17), but we fail to give Him our whole lives. It seems that invariably, there are parts of our lives that need to be put away, but we either fail to see them...or choose not to! Sometimes, we eventually relinquish these lingering qualities ourselves, but other times it takes a friend or loved one or even God Himself to bring them to our attention!

As Easter approaches, let's pray about finding the things in our lives that need to be put away...and let's get the job done!

P.S. I do still have that little blue plaque up...it's okay to think about Christmas for the rest of the winter...right?

Caleb's Birthday Letter

Dear Mom,

For your birthday, you wanted all of us to write you a page of our favorite memories, things you taught us, just some of the things that we will remember you by. At first, I wasn't sure what I was going to write about. I thought, "All the other kids are older and have so much more to look back on." After talking with you in the kitchen some days after school, or hearing you reminisce about memories when we were all still kids or seeing how much you love looking through old pictures of our family to put into your scrapbooks, I can definitely think of plenty that I'm thankful for.

I'm glad that I have you for my Mom. I remember living in Herminie and the basement singing "That Thing You Do," ALL THE TIME! I remember playing Candy Land with you in the living room in Vandergrift. Like I said, I'm not as old as my siblings so most of the things that they remember are things that are happening to me right now. Even though I'm only 17, I can appreciate all the things that you have done and continue to do on a daily basis for me.

You teach me. You taught me simple things...how to walk, talk, read and write; things that I learned as a child. You also taught me things I wouldn't learn at school; manners, civility, and good habits. In a few years I'll be at college and I know that I have you to thank for that. If you hadn't pushed me to work hard in school and get good grades, I wouldn't be where I am today.

What I am most thankful for though, is how much you have cared about me. You want me to excel in everything I do and grow in my faith. And even though sometimes I don't understand why you and Dad say the things that you do, I know that you have my best interests at heart. You have always wanted what's best for me and that's what I am most thankful for.

I know that you say it is hard to watch me grow up because I'm the youngest, but I know that I'll be okay because I've had you as my teacher, my protector and most importantly, my Mom.

I love you. Happy birthday.

Love, Caleb

I Love Decorating

One of the good things about moving every so often (not that I'm hoping to any time in the near future) is that you have a whole new house to decorate! Some people would dread having to do that more than once or twice in their lifetime, but I love it! I enjoy pawing through my eclectic collection of "masterpieces" ...searching for just the right spot to display my treasures...whether it be on a shelf, a wall, or my beautiful mantle. Though I possess no great works of art, nor expensive statues or vases...nothing that would be of value according to the world's standards...the things that I have are priceless...to me!

My shelves are laden with puzzles and games that we've enjoyed together as a family, books that I've practically memorized from reading them so often to the kids, "knick knacks" that I've picked up when shopping with good friends and souvenirs of places we've visited. As I look at my walls, I see the chubby faces of my kids when they were babies, the two of us all dressed in white walking hand in hand down the aisle on that beautiful day in June and our Dads who have gone on before us. I see friends and family, waterfalls, and bridges...some of my favorite things! There are paintings by Chuck, counted cross stitch samplers by me and a plaque declaring that we are a household who serves the Lord (Joshua 24:15).

I guess our possessions tell a story. The story mine tell isn't one of great wealth, but of great love...the love God has for us and that we, in turn, have for each other. They are a testament to the fact that we are truly blessed...and I am so thankful!

Scars

I'm not exactly sure how old I was, maybe seven or eight. I was ice skating at an indoor rink with my cousin. When you ice skate inside, you don't need all of the traditional outerwear, just long pants and a sweater will do. I was a pretty good skater, not that I could do anything fancy, but I'd been skating since I was two, so I could hold my own. However, after making several rounds, I slipped and fell. My cousin was coming up behind me and so he scooped me up and on we went. We made another lap and noticed blood on the ice (not altogether an uncommon sight!). As we came around again, we noticed a second trail of blood. Instinctively, we looked at our hands and that's when I noticed that I was the one bleeding! Evidently, when my cousin was helping me up, he ran over my finger, but I was cold enough that I hadn't felt it. My finger was going to be fine, but my poor fingernail was never to be the same. It split in two (from the top to the bottom) and eventually fell off. When it grew back in, it had a line (or a scar) in it and to this day, if I allow the nail to grow out too far, it will split at the top...an ever reminder of the wound that was mine.

As Easter approaches, I would like to take time to look back at that first Easter and notice the drops of blood...drops of blood that Jesus sweat as He asked the Father to take away His cup of wrath...drops of blood that fell from His back when He was whipped...drops of blood that were brought about by the crown of thorns that was forced upon His head...drops of blood that led all the way to Calvary, where the ultimate blood was shed for our sins as they nailed Him to the cross...drops of blood that were His, this time...not mine...not yours, but His.

Jesus still has His scars, but He doesn't need scars in order to remember...our sins remind Him of why He did what He did...an ever reminder of the wounds that were His. He knew that we could never come to God on our own. He knew that a sacrifice had to be made...and that He was the only one who could make it. He knew that He, being the perfect Son of God, had to die.

Now, so far, this is a pretty depressing story, but it doesn't end there. You see, Jesus didn't stay dead. He rose from the dead on that Easter morning so long ago. He defeated death so that we can live with Him in Heaven someday. There's something else that reminds Jesus of why He did what He did...when a sinner is saved. Jesus did all the work; we just have to believe in Him and accept His gift of salvation!

Newspaper Money

We subscribe to the local newspaper and as the month ended, we owed $6 to our paperboy. While this is a rather small amount of money, it is none the less, desired by him. Since I knew I would be in the middle of preparing dinner when he delivered the paper, I made a check out ahead of time and taped it to the inside of the screen door so that when he delivered the paper, he could retrieve the check.

When he arrived, the door was locked! Not only was he unable to deliver the paper, but the check, fully in sight was unable to be reached. This "dilemma" was easily remedied by a simple knock on the door.

So often we are faced with such dilemmas in our lives, seeing the goal before us, but feeling as though we are unable to reach it. Yet, God is there, ready, willing, and able to give us the desires of our hearts which He has set before us...if we'll only seek Him out!

It is as simply <u>and</u> as hard as that...but worth it all in the end!

Thunderstorms

As we were putting the kids to bed last night, we experienced one of our first thunderstorms of the season. We did all of the usual assuring and reassuring that everything would be all right. Prayers were said, hugs and kisses were exchanged and all the necessary tucking-in was completed.

We no sooner got back downstairs when we heard a loud POP...and out went the lights as well as all the lights in the area. Needless to say, the kids were no longer in bed and we were scrambling to find our oil lamp, candles, and matches. It's amazing how your own house can become like a maze of unknowns with the absence of light. Although it was frustrating trying to find our way around in the dark, we assured the kids that there was no reason to be afraid.

Living your life without the Lord is like trying to find your way in the dark. In John 8:12, Jesus said, "*I am the Light of the world.*" Without His Light in our lives, we are constantly surrounded by spiritual darkness and the things of this world can become very frustrating and even fearsome. Without His Light to guide our steps, we have every reason to be afraid...of the Prince of Darkness...Satan!

So, we finally got the candles lit and the kids back in their beds. It's amazing how one little flame of light can bring so much comfort and peace to an otherwise dark world.

If you're living in spiritual darkness, come to the Light and know the comfort and peace that only Jesus Christ can give!

The Rock

One of the things that we think about at Easter time is the stone being rolled away from the tomb. Technically, I guess, we should call it a rock or even a boulder, for it was definitely more than a stone.

Jesus mentions another rock in Matthew chapter 7, when He refers to the foundation upon which we should build our house. He says it is a foolish person who builds their house on the sand, for when the storms come, the house will be washed away. But it is the wise person who builds their house on the rock, giving it a sound foundation where it can stand up to the storms of life.

Now, not too many of us build houses, but we do build our lives and if we're building our lives on success or popularity or designer clothes or wealth or even other people, we're like the foolish person because those things can't make our lives strong enough to withstand the "storms" that are bound to come our way.

Life promises many trials and tribulations along the way and if we are going to stand strong, we must stand on the Rock – Jesus. He is the only One who can bring us through this life into an eternity with Him in heaven.

So, as Easter comes and you think about that rock outside the tomb, don't forget to think about the Rock inside the tomb – our risen Savior and Lord – the only foundation for a life with Him for eternity.

Fisher Price Farm

I t's never too late to learn something new. When we found out that we were expecting Caleb, we realized that we had almost no baby items left over from our other children. We had no furniture, no clothes, no food-related items, but we did have a few toys, specifically, our Fisher-Price toys. Anyone who is my age or older will remember that the Fisher-Price people used to be "skinny." Sometime, after we had begun quite a collection, they changed over to the "fat" people. Realizing that our toys would no longer be made, we decided to hang onto them.

As Caleb has grown from a baby to a toddler, he has inherited the playground, the school bus, and the famous farm, along with some others. The farm is what I want to focus on.

Back when Charlie, Carrie and Caitlin were young, I wouldn't be able to tell you how much they played with that farm. I couldn't begin to count the times I helped the cow and the horse to stand on all four legs and showed the kids how to put the animals' heads down into the feeding trough. I showed them how to put the harness on the horse and told them that either the horse or the tractor could pull the wagon. If they played with it outside, I remember telling them that, "No, the pig doesn't need to go in <u>real</u>

mud," and "No, you don't have to pull up <u>real</u> grass for the sheep to eat." "Yes, the boy and girl are allowed to play in the loft, but they must stay back from the edge so they don't fall and get hurt." "No, the Mom doesn't have to stay in the kitchen all day," and "Yes, she'd love to have a turn at driving the tractor, too. In fact, she'll probably get the job done more quickly because she likes to drive faster than your Dad, I mean <u>the</u> Dad!" You see, this wasn't just some kid's toy, it was an interactive teaching tool!

Anyway, I considered myself an authority on the Fisher-Price farm, so when it came time to get it out for Caleb, I was ready to go! One day, he was sitting in his highchair, playing with the chicken and the rooster and I noticed that they have little square holes in their bottoms. I realized that I'd seen them before, but I found myself wondering why those holes were there. (Some of you may already be ahead of me here!) Suddenly, it dawned on me: those holes are there so that the chicken and the rooster can "roost" up on top of the fence posts. Charlie was there when I had my "epiphany" and neither one of us could believe that after all those years, we had never noticed that! We were so excited with this new discovery!

Reading the Bible is, often times, like that. I can't begin to tell you how many times I've read through the Bible, but sometimes I'll read a passage that I've obviously read before and it's as if I'm reading it for the first time! I have an "epiphany" and that verse takes on a whole new meaning...and I am always so excited!

No, it's never too late to learn something new...so keep reading your Bible over and over and be amazed at the new things that God has to teach you!

Tub Job

We are in the process of having the wall around the bathtub fixed. When it's all done, the tub will be the same, but the wall will be one of those "tub surround" units. Just to prove my ignorance of such affairs, I thought that he would bring in the new unit, plop it down right over the existing tile and "poof," we'd be done. How naïve of me! He has ripped out the tiles, exposing the wet wall behind, insulated, cut boards to go over that, spackled once with two more spackling rounds to come. After that, I think the wall unit will be installed. Obviously, this is a much bigger and longer job than I expected.

So, what's the point of my telling you this? Being a Christian is a constant journey, an endless process of becoming more like Christ. Occasionally, He makes some necessary changes in us immediately, literally overnight. However, many of the changes which Christ desires to make in us take time, lots of time. We gradually become more like Christ, according to God's methods and timing. He doesn't just cover over the sin in our lives. He gets rid of it and then He insulates us against the Devil's schemes and then He spackles and patches, building a strong foundation for our new "look." Finally, the job is complete and we are once again useful to Him.

The key to enduring our "tub job" is patience. Also, there is the expectation of the joy of a shower which is both useful and free from flaws. So goes our Christian walk. We must be patient as God works in our lives, ever changing us to be more like Christ. Also, we have the expectation of the joy we shall experience when God is finished with us and we are useful to Him and free from the flaws of sin.

Weeds

Last year, we transplanted seven rose bushes from various parts of the yard to a "bed" in the backyard. They made it through the winter and even bloomed this spring. Unfortunately, between taking care of Caleb and doing all of the everyday things, I neglected to tend to the rose bushes. Recently, while I was hanging clothes on the line, I took a good look at the rose bushes and noticed that they were in dire need of pruning, weeding and of course, watering and feeding.

It's amazing how the lack of rain can hurt our grass and flowers, but the weeds continue to flourish. The bushes were surrounded by all of the usual weeds; however, the biggest problem was

Left untended, sin will eventually choke the spiritual life right out of us!

that morning glories had wound around the stems of those rose bushes.

Morning glories appear to be harmless, even pretty, yet I was amazed at how tightly they had wound themselves around the roses, choking the life out of them. It was difficult to break the grip that they had on the roses. In fact, the roses even put up a fight (and I have the scratches to prove it!), but finally, the morning glories were gone and the roses looked so much better.

Satan is like those morning glories. He ever so slowly wraps sin around us, charming us with flowers along the way, until we are so intertwined that we can't break free. In fact, we get so used to it being there, that when God comes to set us free, we fight Him (and He has the scars to prove it!)

Left untended, that sin will eventually choke the spiritual life right out of us! How thankful we can be that God is a much better gardener than I am. As long as we don't fight Him, He is willing to feed, water and weed daily, pruning whenever necessary.

How I'm Remembered

If I were to say: "The Gettysburg Address" or "Honest Abe," you'd say: "Things we remember about Abraham Lincoln. "The Father of our Country" would, of course, be George Washington. If I were to mention the song, "Just As I Am," you would probably think of Billy Graham, especially if I mentioned the word "crusade." If we remembered the maker of our first flag, we'd be remembering Betsy Ross. A giant killer with a sling would remind us of the would-be king of Israel, David. I could go on and on, but the point is that we use words and phrases to remember things about people-whether they're famous or not. For instance, if I mentioned "tractor rides" to my three older children, they would say "Papa."

Recently, I went to a funeral where the people in attendance had the opportunity to come forward and share some words of remembrance about the deceased. This really caused me to think: How will I be remembered? What words will people use to describe my life? Oh, we all have good and bad things that we could be remembered by. For example, my kids could say, "She was always after us to make our beds and pick up after ourselves." Hopefully, they'd find something more important to remember, like "She always read the Bible to us when we were small and then encouraged us to do it on our own when we were older. She enjoyed teaching Sunday School and taught all of us at one time or another. She loved playing games with us and always gave us new ones at Christmas." My husband could surely remember being "nagged" a time or two (grin), but hopefully he'd think of me as the wife who was totally devoted to him from the time we met.

We all hope that people will remember the good things about us. So, we need to make sure that the good things are the most memorable things and that the most memorable things are the things that really matter. In other words, we need to make our lives count for something.

Ideally, I hope that people remember me as someone whose faith in Jesus Christ was made evident by the way she lived her life. And...that is my hope for all of you as well.

Epilogue

While I went for a walk this morning, I asked the Lord to help me understand better the passing of my sweet wife, Cheryl. While I do not claim to have heard a voice, I believe I was led to think the following and as I share these thoughts, I mean no disrespect to my Savior or the written Word of God.

The disciples absolutely loved Jesus. He lived with them. He loved them, yet it was inevitable that He was going to leave them. He was going to die. However, Jesus shared with them that once He was gone from this earth, He would send One who would make possible that the Gospel would go forth into the world, that His presence, the Holy Spirit, would be able to do far more and reach more people than if Jesus remained on the earth. Jesus' words have proven to be true.

Like I stated above, I mean no disrespect and of course, my wife is not Jesus, but I liken her story to His.

I absolutely loved Cheryl. She lived with me and she loved me and so many others, yet it was inevitable that she was going to leave us. She was going to die. However, her death has made it possible for two books to be written of her experiences with family and the strong love of Jesus that would not have been possible if she were still with us here today.

Cheryl has been able to reach 100s perhaps 1000s more with a message of hope and the promise of salvation in Christ than if she remained on earth and that has proven to be true.

I am sure the disciples of Jesus missed Him terribly when He was gone even though the Gospel was being shared around the world. I know that I miss Cheryl terribly now that she is gone even though the Gospel is being shared with her writings around the world.

Her legacy is precious and far reaching. As the disciples longed for the day to be reunited with their Savior, I look forward to the day to be in His presence and to be reunited with this wonderful woman of God who has pointed many others to Jesus.

What will be your legacy? Will others desire to see Jesus because of the life you have lived on this earth?

May you honor God with your life so that others can know the Savior, not only while you are here on earth, but even more so when you are gone.

Look to Jesus, my friend. Trust your life to Him today so that others can know of Him now and in the days to come.

Chuck

While this is the end of this book, it is not the end of the story. Share this book and our website with friends and family to keep Cheryl's stories going.

If you enjoyed this collection of Ponderings, please consider donating to help us publish the 3rd installment of Cheryl's writings, "Ponderings – A Devotional Guide".

More information is available at:

www.PonderingsFromThePastorsPartner.com

Thank you and God Bless!